Margaret Oliphant

The Fugitives (in Good Cheer)

Margaret Oliphant

The Fugitives (in Good Cheer)

ISBN/EAN: 9783741192296

Manufactured in Europe, USA, Canada, Australia, Japa

Cover: Foto ©Thomas Meinert / pixelio.de

Manufactured and distributed by brebook publishing software
(www.brebook.com)

Margaret Oliphant

The Fugitives (in Good Cheer)

"*Good words are worth much and cost little.*"—*Herbert.*

GOOD WORDS

FOR 1879

EDITED BY

DONALD MACLEOD, D.D.,

ONE OF HER MAJESTY'S CHAPLAINS FOR SCOTLAND

And illustrated by

MRS. BLACKBURN ("J. B."), J. McL. RALSTON, G. G. KILBURNE.
J. E. CHRISTIE, A. S. BOYD, F. DADD, A. J. C. HARE,
R. T. PRITCHETT, AND OTHERS

LONDON
ISBISTER AND COMPANY
LIMITED
56, LUDGATE HILL
1879

CHRISTMAS COMES BUT ONCE A YEAR
& WHEN IT COMES IT BRINGS GOOD CHEER.

'OOD CHEER'

CHRISTMAS, 1879.

THE FUGITIVES.

CHAPTER I.

H ELEN GOULBURN was sitting alone in the great drawing-room of her father's country house on an evening in October. It had been very sultry during the day, and the great heat had ended in a thunderstorm and torrents of rain. Now all the tumult and commotion of the elements were over. The night was cool and fresh. The great windows were open to the unseen garden, from which a sweetness of honeysuckle and mignonette and late roses came in upon every breath of the fitful night air. The room was an immense room, far too large for a solitary occupant. She and her lamp and her white dress made a lightness in one corner; the rest of the huge drawing-room was faintly lighted with candles, of which there were regiments about on the walls, reflected vaguely from mirrors here and there, on tables and consoles and cabinets—but yet not enough to give anything like light to the vast shadowy room, which was full of everything that is rich and rare—of everything at least that the highest price could buy or the best workmen produce. The windows, a long line of them, all draped in that shadowy whiteness, stood open, as has been said. Most girls of Helen's age would have been afraid to sit all alone, with so many windows opening on to a lawn, which in its turn swept downwards into the park, at so late an hour. Sometimes the lace curtains swayed in the night wind as if put aside by a shadowy hand. It was difficult to keep the imagination from developing some stealthy figure half hidden in the drapery, some one coming in, out of the darkness outside. The house was full of wealth, and the temptations to a sudden raid might have been many. When the branches swayed on the night air, bringing down a shower of raindrops, or some twig cracked, or one of the mysterious noises of which darkness is always full, broke the absolute quiet, any one of those sounds, which yet were scarcely definite sounds at all, might have conveyed a tremor to the lonely occupant of all this mystic space and solitude. But Helen sat unmoved. She was used to the vacant bigness of the great house, often inhabited by only herself and her little sister, and a crowd of servants. She had been in the hands of a governess till very lately, and in the routine of lessons and the certainty that a school-girl was not likely to be interrupted by visitors, had escaped all consciousness of the isolation of the great house. It was the most splendid in the county, surrounded by a beautiful park, embosomed in great trees. When Mr. Goulburn bought it from the decaying proud family to whom its glories belonged, Fareham was already a noble place; and he had added greatly to it, had built out a room here and a room there, and enlarged it with every extravagance of convenience that lavish wealth could think of. He had built and decorated in the most costly way the splendid room in which his daughter was sitting; he had fitted out for her a suite of rooms worthy of a princess; the very servants were lodged as half the well-to-do people in England would have been glad to be lodged. Outside, in the darkness of the summer night, full of dew and rain and soft fragrance, were acres of flower-beds and conservatories, tended by a regiment of gardeners.

But notwithstanding all this splendour, the county looked very shyly on the new member of its sacred and select society. He had brought very good introductions, and he gave such dinners as were not to be had within a hundred miles. The Duke called, an honour scarcely less than royal condescension; but the surrounding gentry showed no enthusiasm in following that example. Helen was then still in the school-room, which furnished the ladies with a very good excuse; but even after the ball which was given on the occasion of her coming out, and which certified that event to all the world, no genial circle of neighbours collected round her. Even her youth, her solitude, her motherless and friendless condition, did not call forth the sympathy of the county people. Never was girl more solitary. Her governess, who it had been arranged was to stay with her as chaperon, had married suddenly the widowed vicar of the parish, and deserted her not long before the period of which we speak: and she was left alone, the mistress of the wealthiest, most barren, and splendid house in all the district. She had crowds of servants to do whatever she bade —carriages, horses, whatever, as the servants'

hall said, heart could desire—but no friends. Little Jane, her little sister, was the offspring of a marriage which her father had made "abroad," and of which, except this child, no trace existed. It was only on his return with the baby, six years before, that his extraordinary wealth had shown itself. Before that period Helen had been left at a school in the country—but not in this part of the country —where she had been happy enough with her companions. But when her father returned from "abroad," everything had been changed for her. An ayah had brought the baby home, and Helen had first become aware of the existence of a little sister when she saw a big pair of dark eyes gleaming out of the palest of little faces over the dusky nurse's shoulder. She had been taken away from her school from that day, and ever since had lived the life of a princess, waited upon by innumerable servants, and living in luxurious houses. But her father had always lived the life of a bachelor, notwithstanding his possession of these two daughters. His friends had been all men. There were great dinners now and then, and occasionally Helen had seen through an open door a glimpse of a long splendid table laden with plate and crystal, and baskets of fruit and flowers, where her father's friends were being entertained. But no ladies had come to the house, nor, after the childish companions of her school, had she had any friends in her new magnificence, except Miss Temple, who had been very good to her, and whose departure had brought a poignant sensation of loss into the girl's mind. It was almost the only keen feeling she had ever known. She had come into society with something of the bewildered, uncertain vision of a creature bred in the darkness who is dazzled and confused rather than delighted by the light. The people who came to the ball had been as figures in a dream to her. The whole scene was like something in the theatre. She was scarcely aware that she was herself not a spectator, but an actor in it, walking about mechanically among the guests, making her mechanical curtsey when her father brought up, now one strange face, now another.

And after that one ball, silence had fallen again upon Fareham. The porter at the lodge received sheaves of cards, and some carriages even penetrated through the grand avenue to the hall door; but no one entered the house. Doubtless there were some hearts in those carriages in which there vibrated some touch of pity for the millionaire's shy, motherless, inexperienced daughter. But the

GOOD CHEER.

Page 3.

county was wonderfully intact, and its gentry had made up their minds to discourage the advent of Money among them. A few years of perseverance would no doubt have made an end of that irrational notion; but in the meantime they distrusted Mr. Goulburn. He was far too rich; it was insolent of a man who, so far as any one knew, was nobody, to be richer than all the squires put together. A ball in such a house might be tolerated. It was like a public ball; you took your own party (for in this respect the invitations were most liberal), and, save that one of your men had to sacrifice himself to ask the girl of the house to dance once, you kept yourselves to yourselves, as you did at the ball' for the hospital or any other subscription assembly. This was what the county people said. And as for Helen, she was often dull, but she had not learned to blame anybody for her dulness. She thought it a law of nature—it was no one's fault.

All this explanation is to show how it was that Helen found nothing unusual in her own position, alone in this great dim room, with all the windows open. The windows always were open, except in the depth of winter. The darkness without had no dangers for her; it never occurred to her that any strange apparition might disturb her solitude. She liked the stillness, the night air, the fragrance from the garden. Though she usually went to bed early, yet on this night she was not sleepy. She was reading a novel; that was one of the luxuries which her father provided regularly. She had not read many books that were worth reading, but of novels all kinds. When the butler came softly into the room, with the intention of closing up the house for the night, she stopped him.

"Are you going to sit up to-night, Brownlow?" she said.

"Yes, Miss Goulburn, as usual on Saturdays, till the last train comes in," the man replied.

"Then leave the windows open a little longer."

"Yes, Miss Goulburn," he said. But he did not go away forthwith; he extinguished the candles on the distant tables and in the sconces, moving like a shadow (though he was very substantial) in that elegant desert of costly furniture, until finally Helen's figure in her white dress, lit up by her lamp, became the one definite point in the darkness. She was at some distance from the windows, in the winter corner near the fireplace, now all dark. Everything was dark except that one

spot. The soft and almost stealthy closing of the door was all that testified to Brownlow's departure; he had become invisible before. In the great stillness his soft and regular step, subdued and respectful, as a good servant's ought to be, yet stately, was heard retiring, thick though the carpets were and closely fitting every door. He went away through those softly carpeted corridors and across the great marble hall to his own part of the house. And once more absolute silence and solitude abode with Helen. The night air came in softly, swaying the curtains; sometimes a bough creaked, a long tendril of some creeping plant shook out a few raindrops, a moth dashed against the panes. No other sound in heaven or earth. And Helen in her white dress gave a heart to the darkness. All alone, no one near her, yet not afraid!

CHAPTER II.

What was it that stirred?

Scarcely a sound at all—not half so definite as the cracking of the twigs, the boom of the night moth against the window; yet it affected Helen as those sounds never did. When it had occurred twice she raised her head. It was nothing, and yet—— Again! What was it? Though you would not call it a sound it made the air thrill as no sound of the inanimate ever does. She looked up, but the light of her own lamp blinded her. She could scarcely see beyond its charmed circle. Then a slight jar succeeded to the soft pressure, as of a human foot upon the turf. A sound that conveys purpose and energy, how different is it from the aimless noises of nature! She rose up in great, though restrained alarm, with a cry almost on her lips. Then Helen reflected that all the servants were far away, that a scream would not help her much; and though her heart beat wildly, almost taking from her both sight and hearing, she still could after a sort both hear and see. She stood up, closely drawn against the wall, looking out with puckered eyelids. Then a hand stole between the curtains of the nearest window: they were pushed aside, and a dark figure showed itself, at first indistinguishable, a something merely, an emblem of mystery and danger. Helen's scream got vent, but in a low cry only of fright and dismay. Then all at once the fluttering of her heart stopped, her pulses regained their steadiness.

"Papa!" she said, "oh, how you have frightened me! Why didn't you come in the other way?" It was a great relief, for her terror had been all the greater that she had never experienced any visionary alarms before, and her imagination was unprepared. She put out her hand to the bell, " I will ring for Brownlow——"

Her father did not leave her time even for another word. He sprang forward and caught her arm. "Don't do anything of the kind," he said. "I want no Brownlow. I am going again immediately. I want no one. I don't wish it to be known that I have been here."

It was certainly her father, but not the placid, prosperous, moneyed man she knew. His coat, which was of a rough kind she had never seen him wear before, was beaded with rain. His face was pale and haggard; his dress bore traces of mud as if he had scrambled over ditches; his boots were wet and clogged with the damp soil. She looked at him with a terror she could not express, and he looked at her with a somewhat stern inquiry in his eyes.

"But you are wet: you want—dinner—something?" she faltered. "Shall I run and bid them bring——"

He shook her slightly, still holding her arm. "Are you good for anything?" he said. 'Have you any stuff in you? Now is the time to test it. Go and get that white rag off. Put on your darkest dress, and come with me."

"Come with you? To-night, papa?"

He gave her a slight shake again. "It will neither be to-night or any other night if you make so much noise. What are you capable of, Helen? Are you able to be quick, and silent, and brave? Can I rely upon you?—if not say so; but make up your mind, for there is not a moment to lose."

She grew whiter than her white dress, and looked at him with gleaming, wide open eyes. She had read of appeals like this, but she could not remember how the heroines responded. She said, faltering, "I can be quick, and quiet, papa."

"That is all that is necessary; but we have not a moment's time to lose. No one must know that I have been here. I shall go out again outside the window and wait for you. Go up to my room to the little Italian cabinet near my bed, on the right hand. You know it, and you know how to open the secret drawer? Here is the key, bring me a little portfolio, a sort of letter case you will find in it. Stop; that is not all. Change your dress and put on thick boots, and a cloak, and a veil. Then go and bring Janey——"

"Janey! papa? She has been in bed for hours."

"Did I say she was not in bed? Take up the child out of her bed, wrap her in something, and bring her down-stairs. You can surely carry that little thing down-stairs. After that I'll take charge of her myself."

"But, papa, Janey! she is so little. If I wake her she will cry."

"Not she! But why wake her at all? Lift her, and wrap her in something warm; she need not be awake. My poor little Janey! I can't go without my Janey," he said to himself.

Helen scarcely knew what she was saying in her consternation and surprise. "If you are going anywhere, papa, and want to take Janey—at this hour—would it not be best to order the brougham?"

"Would it not be best to order a coach and six, with half-a-dozen fools to draw it?" he said savagely. Just then some far-off sounds were audible, some one moving in the silence of the house. Mr. Goulburn made a hurried step towards the window. Then paused and said in a half-whisper which he seemed to try to make tender, "Let me see what mettle you are made of, Helen. Do what I have told you without betraying yourself—without attracting any one's attention. Show what you are good for, once in your life."

He disappeared, and Helen stood for a moment like one in a dream. Was it a dream? and would she awake?—or had the rest of her life been a dream to which this was the awaking? She felt that her father was watching her from behind the white mist of the curtains, and that she dared not delay. She went up-stairs mechanically. The huge house lay silent like an enchanted palace. On Saturdays it was always possible that the master might return by the late train, and it was common for the great household of servants, badly ruled and prodigal, to hold a sort of domestic saturnalia on that night. Faint sounds of fun and frolic were to be heard from the servants' hall—very faint, for Brownlow had a sense of his responsibilities —and all the guardians of the place were out of the way. Helen went up, unseen and solitary, to her father's room and her own. She did what he had told her—changed her own dress, and took the Russia leather letter-case, which was full apparently of papers, out of the secret drawer of the cabinet. But there she paused; the other part of the mission was more difficult; and Helen stood still again, with a beating heart, outside the door of little Janey's nursery, where the nurse certainly ought to be, even if all the other servants were off duty. What should she do if the nurse were there! Her mission was difficult enough without that. When Helen went in, however, to the luxurious rooms appropriated to her little sister, no nurse was visible. The child of the millionaire slept, unwatched, like the child of the poorest clerk. A faint night-light burnt in the inner room. There were acres of stairs and corridors between little Janey and the highly-paid functionary who was supposed to be devoted to her body and soul. She might have died of fright before any one could have heard her cry. Helen stood, breathless, at the foot of the little bed in which Janey lay fast asleep. She thought she had never realised before what perfect rest was, or the beauty of the child who lay with her pretty round arms thrown above her head, rosy with sleep and warmth, her soft breathing making a little murmurous cadence in the stillness. How can I have the heart to wake her? Helen said to herself; a new sentiment, half tenderness, half fear, seemed to awaken in her heart. To wake the little one to this hurried incomprehensible night journey seemed terrible—yet somehow Helen felt a reluctant conviction that Janey would adapt herself to the adventure better than she herself should. The child's sleep, however, was so profound, and there was something so contrary to all the prejudices of education in waking her up at that hour, that only the thought of her father's severe and haggard countenance kept Helen to her errand. She had even turned away to go back to him—to say that she could not do it—when the greater evil of having to return again, and of, perhaps, meeting the nurse next time, prevailed. She got a warm little pelisse, with many capes—a piquant little Parisian garment, which had tantalized all the mothers in the district—out of its drawer, and put the little shoes ready. Then she bent over her small sister and called her. "Janey, wake up, wake up; papa wants you. Wake up; we are to go with him if you are quiet and don't cry."

The child sat up in her bed, awake all at once, with big, dark eyes, opening like windows in her pale face. "I am not doing to cry," she said, and stared at her sister through the gloom which was faintly illuminated by the night-lamp. Janey was, as Helen had anticipated, much more at home in the emergency than she was. She woke up in a moment as children do, not with a margin of bewilderment and confusion such as is common to us—but wide awake, with all her little intelligence fresh and on the alert.

"What is it? what is it, Helen?"

"I don't know; but you are to go down to papa. You are to be quiet; you are not to cry. We are going with him."

"Where? where?"

"I don't know," said Helen, ready to weep with the strange and wild confusion, the sense of misery and wretchedness which was involved to her in this overthrowal of all habits, this sudden secrecy and adventure in the dark. But little Janey clapped her hands. It was a delightful novelty to the child. She pulled on her stockings on her own small pink feet, her eyes dancing with pleasure and excitement. No need to carry her down asleep, as Helen with terror and doubt of her own powers had feared.

"You must be quiet; you must be quiet—not to let the servants know," the elder sister whispered.

"I am doing to be quiet," said the little girl, delighted with the mystery. She thrust her big doll into her little bed, and covered it carefully, while Helen, not knowing what she did, picked up various fugitive articles, half-consciously, and put them into the pockets of the ulster which she had put on.

"Be dood, baby, and keep my little bed warm till I come back," sang little Janey.

"Oh, hush, hush! you are to be quiet—you are to be quiet," Helen said.

They crept down the great stairs like two ghosts, fantastic little shadows, so unlike anything that could have been expected on that grand staircase at that hour. But they met no one. The sounds from the servants' hall were a little more audible as the evening went on. The master was absent, the master's daughter too shy and timid, even had she heard them, to take any notice. The hours of license were approaching when even Mr. Brownlow relaxed the bonds of discipline. As these sounds reached them little Janey clasped her sister's hand tighter. But it was the sense of a mischievous escapade, not of a mysterious calamity, which was in her mind.

"What will Nursey say?" the child said with a low laugh.

Even the whisper frightened Helen. The lights flared in all those vacant passages, but gloom lurked in every corner; the great rooms were all dark and empty, not a living being, not a sound of habitation was in the magnificent costly place, except the squeak of the footman's violin, the far-off laughter of the servants—so much for so little! Amid all the confusion and terror of the moment, Helen always recollected the vacant lighted staircase, the hall with its marble pillars, the vast darkness of the dining-room standing open—not a creature near, except those two helpless creatures equipped for flight; but on the other hand, the servants' merry-making, and the squeak of the fiddle painfully scratching out a popular tune. They paused to listen for one moment, holding their breath. Then they went into the drawing-room, where Helen's lamp was still burning close to the wall, making the darkness visible. Her book was still lying open on the table. She had left the heroine at a painful crisis, but it was not so terrible as this.

Helen closed the door behind her with great precautions, and Janey, a little frightened at the dark, clung to her closely.

"Where is papa? I don't see papa," cried the child.

"Oh, hush, hush !" said Helen, frightened by the sound of her voice.

He was standing behind the curtains waiting for them.

"How long you have been !" he said to her in a low, stern voice; but he opened his arms to the child. "My little Janey—my little darling !" he said, bending down on his knees to bring himself within her reach. Janey clasped her arms round his neck, and kissed him, with open-mouthed, childish kisses.

"Where are you doing to take me, papa?" she said, her dark eyes dancing with excitement. He raised himself up, holding her closely clasped to his breast, and carried her out into the night.

What a strange night-walk it was—through the country lanes, all heavy and muddy after the storm, and dark as the darkest midnight; brushing against the rustling, thorny hedges, stumbling over heaps of stones, through the pools at the roadside, and upon the slippery grass; here and there crossing a stile, at haphazard, with no guide but instinct; here stealing past a cottage, shrinking from the lamps of the doctor's gig, which threw a suspicious light upon them. Helen, following, dragging her weary feet through the muddy ways, holding up the long skirts not intended for such usage in her arms, her veil over her face, felt herself shrink, too, when the light flashed upon them. But who could have supposed that it was the master of Fareham and his children that were out there in the muddy lanes? Once at the turnpike, where they were all as well known as the day, her father, whom she always saw before her, a vague, dark shadow with the child in his arms, replied in a gruff feigned voice, with a fictitious country accent which

gave Helen a sharp shock, to the good-night of the gatekeeper. To avoid notice was one thing, to tell a practical lie was another. This, in the midst of her confused wretchedness, gave her a painful prick of sensation. Janey in her excitement had begun to prattle at first, but had been summarily silenced by her father, and now drooped upon his shoulder fast asleep, her face half hidden in the rough collar of his coat. Between the other two not a word passed. Helen was too miserable and too much bewildered to ask any questions; she followed submissively.

The little station was within about a mile of Fareham, but a mile is long when trudged through mud and rain by unaccustomed feet, in a gloomy night, and with a heavy heart. A late train going express to town which otherwise would have scorned this little station, had been arranged to stop there for the convenience of the man of business, the well-known Mr. Goulburn, whose affairs were on too colossal a scale to be managed by the ordinary means of communication open to everybody. Sometimes he had special parcels to send by the guard : sometimes a clerk who had "run down" for some special directions, or an associate acting with him on some great city board, whose time was too valuable to permit the loss of a moment, took advantage of this train; and sometimes he himself, jumping into a dog-cart the moment the latest guest had departed after a sumptuous dinner, had rushed up to town by it. The station-master and the porters were like his own servants, and the whole place all but kept for his convenience. He crept up to it now, keeping carefully in the shadow, out of the glare of its poor paraffin lamps.

"Keep yourself muffled up, and your veil down, and go and get the tickets," Mr. Goulburn said in the low and peremptory tone in which he had throughout addressed Helen. She went without a word ; she who had never in her life done any such thing for herself. The clerk peered at her through his wicket; the solitary porter stared as she stood alone on the little platform. She was left there alone until the train came up, and the three persons who formed the *personnel* of the station had nothing to do but to stare at her, and ask about the luggage which she did not possess. When the train stopped with its usual little fret and commotion, Mr. Goulburn suddenly came forward and plunged into an empty carriage. His high coat-collar, the slouch of his hat, and finally the figure of the child asleep upon his shoulder, concealed him effectually. Helen could not help wondering whether she was as effectually disguised, and the thought once more gave her a sharp pinch of pain. Why were they hiding themselves? There was not a word spoken while the train rushed on, tearing through that darkness which they had just traversed so slowly and painfully. Only once, and that when they were but just started, did any communication pass between the father and daughter. They both looked out towards the home they had left, though it was invisible as they left the little station. Upon the road close by the lights of a carriage were visible, slowly approaching. It was the carriage which, when Mr. Goulburn was absent, was dispatched to meet the last train on Saturday nights. The last train from London was not due for half an hour, and the coachman came along at a leisurely pace, slowly climbing the road to meet his master, who was flying, disguised and shameful, in the other direction. The contrast was so strange that he looked at Helen, and their eyes met. Something piteous was in his look. It contained a whole world of misery, of consciousness, of appeal which was almost humorous, amidst the profundity of pain. She had asked no questions, she had scarcely ventured to form to herself an idea of what the cause of this flight could be, but for the first time her heart was touched.

"Does she not tire you, lying on your shoulder? I could take her a little, papa," she said. She could think of no other way of showing her sympathy. He shook his head and pressed the child closer to him. Was it that the touch of her innocence made him feel less guilty? Was it that to convince himself of the strength of the natural affection in him made him think himself a better man? or was it only the one real and true sentiment which may still preserve the least worthy from perdition? Helen looked somewhat wistfully at her little sister, lying in all the *abandon* of childish sleep, helpless yet omnipotent, across her father's breast. She had never been a favourite like little Janey. No passion of parental affection had ever been lavished upon her, and, in consequence, she knew her father better, and perhaps secretly trusted him less, than children ought to do—though she had never said this even to herself. But, for the moment, she sitting close opposite to them, carried off from all her anchors, swept into some wild sea of the unknown, looked at them wistfully, and envied the father and the child.

In a few hours more Helen understood much more perfectly what the metaphor meant which we have just employed. At midnight they embarked in a steamer which, after threading its way down the river through a thousand dangers, plunged into the Channel just as daybreak made the rough waves and flying foam visible. It was a small, old, almost worn-out boat, and the voyage was one of the longer and cheaper ones which tempt passengers from the ordinary routes, to their profound suffering and repentance. Helen had never been at sea before. She lay trembling while the vessel creaked and plunged, not knowing what to reply to Janey's inquiry, why the ship went up and down. Why, indeed? it seemed to do so on purpose, tossing them up one moment and down the other with that sickening repetition which helps to make up the agony of a voyage to the inexperienced. In the morning, in the perplexing and painful daylight of which Helen felt afraid, she did not know why, they landed on foreign soil. Her father had changed during the night, she could not tell how. Was it possible that already on the previous evening he had worn the large whiskers and carefully smoothed hair which seemed to have grown lighter, redder, than it used to be? She scarcely knew him when he came on deck, and he gave her an uneasy look when he met her eye. She did not, however, suspect the truth as yet, nor did she in the least understand his disguise. She was only full of alarm and wonder, not knowing what to think.

CHAPTER III.

"WHERE are we going, papa?" Helen had walked some way, bewildered and wondering, through the foreign streets, confused by the strange language round her, the unfamiliar look of everything, the strangeness of her situation altogether. They had set out walking, and seemed, she thought, to be going on vaguely from street to street without any aim, passing hotel after hotel, at any of which she would have been glad to rest and collect her thoughts after the rough voyage and all the agitations of the night. "Where are you going to take us, papa?" said little Janey, running along by his side. The child was pale too, and her pretty, costly clothes had already acquired that look of crumpled finery which garments too good for common use so easily assume. Helen, too, had found it very difficult to manage her dress, with its train, made for no greater exertion than to sweep over the velvet lawns at Fareham. It had dropped from her hand now and then. It had got crushed and crumpled and a little soiled with the wet deck. It looked like a dress that had been worn all night. The signs of the night journey and rough sea were unmistakable upon them. Mr. Goulburn made no reply. He murmured something to soothe the little girl, but made no answer to Helen. Their questions, however, seemed to rouse him to action. He went into a shop which was full of *articles de voyage*, and there bought a large second-hand portmanteau considerably battered, and one of those iron-bound trunks which are used by Continental travellers. Then he put a purse into Helen's hand, and took her to the door of another shop, in which were exhibited all kinds of feminine apparel. "Buy what is wanted for yourself and *her*," he said. Helen had scarcely ever in her life so much as entered a shop alone, but necessity overcomes everything, even the shy inexperience of a girl. She went in submissively, trembling to face the brisk saleswomen, all her schoolroom French deserting her in this earliest emergency. Nevertheless, she managed to do what was absolutely essential. As for Janey, she proved herself much more a woman of the world than her elder sister. The whole adventure was a frolic to Janey—a frolic which the voyage had unpleasantly interrupted, but which had regained its jollity and excitement. She made her choice among the different dresses exhibited to them with unfailing promptitude. "I am doing to have this," she said in her childish peremptory tone, to the great delight of the shopwomen, who gathered round her, offering her all their wares. The little English child, recovering all the vivacity of her childish spirits, and excited by the laughter and flatteries, though she did not understand them, of the French milliners, was an amusing little figure, and the scene like a scene in a comedy. Janey inspected all the garments, feeling the texture with her baby fingers, assuming a hundred little airs of importance. She chattered without ceasing, a perpetual flood of remarks, while the women laughed and admired.

"What does she say?" they asked the one among them who partially justified the "Ici on parle Anglais" in the shop-window. "Elle est délicieuse," the shopwoman said; "elle est jolie comme un cœur: et d'un goût!"

Janey did not understand a word, but all the same knew she was being applauded, and her little head was turned by the notice bestowed upon her. "We came without any boxes or frocks or anything, and papa is doing to let me buy whatever I like," said Janey.

The women were curious beyond description when this was rapidly reported to them by the one who understood. All this strange little scene went on while Helen, still half dazed, stammered out her orders in her faltering, imperfect French, and accepted timidly what was offered to her. The colour came to her cheeks, and a painful prick of life to her being, when she heard her little sister's indiscreet explanation. "We left all our things behind—by mistake," she said, trembling, a tingling, smarting blush dyeing her face. The timid falsehood redoubled her own confusion, but it did not do much more. It changed, Helen thought, the looks of the women. They followed her about, she fancied, trying to elicit further revelations from Janey, pressing every kind of outfit upon her; watching her as if—— What did they imagine? Did they think she would steal something? Helen's heart swelled so in her simplicity that she thought it would burst. She held Janey's hand closely in her own, and squeezed it tight. "Don't talk so, don't talk so," she whispered. And then asked herself, with an indescribable pang, why should not the child talk? A grey light of knowledge, a vague, miserable twilight of consciousness, like the first lightening of a gloomy dawn, was stealing over her. When she had made her purchases—two frocks for Janey, the simplest which that little heroine could be prevailed on to accept, and a plain dark dress for herself, and a supply of underclothing—she found her father at the door, with the box he had bought upon a cab. This was how they were provided with the luggage which is indispensable to respectability. Helen could not but look at him with different eyes, now that she felt herself a party to this fraud, which she began to be conscious of, without knowing what it meant. What did it mean? Almost involuntarily unawares had not she herself made a false statement in explanation of the extraordinary straits in which they were? She watched her father, and found him changed, she could scarcely tell how. His hair had changed its colour; his beard had grown miraculously in a single night. What did it mean? Her heart ached with the question, but she did not know how to reply.

He took them to the railway after this—to the railway again, after all their past fatigue. He was not negligent, however, of their com-

fort, but made them eat at the buffet, and took a *coupé* for them, filling it with all the picture-books and papers he could find, with baskets of fruit and chocolate and bonbons. " Here is a corner where my little Janey can go to sleep," he said, putting the child tenderly into it when the train had started. Janey jumped upon his knee, and began to chatter and give him an account of her own achievements at the shop.

" They understood me," said the little thing, " better than Helen. I can't speak French, but they understood me better than Helen. Papa, do you hear? they understood me—" Here she paused and gave a sudden cry. She had a pretty way of calling the attention of the careless listener, drawing his face round with her little hand upon his chin. " Papa!" she said in great alarm, " you have dot hair on your chin, and it moves. Oh! papa!"

His face grew crimson. He turned the child from his knee, giving her a sudden sharp blow on the cheek with his open hand —a blow which was nothing, yet like a revolution of earth and heaven to Janey, and to Helen too. Then, muttering a curse under his breath, he turned to Helen, who was watching him, pale with terror and wonder and indignation. " Well!" he said defiantly,

" out with it. You are a spy upon me too. Let me hear what you have got to say."

" I have nothing to say, papa," said Helen, trembling. She looked at him wistfully with miserable insight in her eyes. She saw now that it was all false—hair and complexion and even expression. It seemed to her, as she looked at him, that it was not her father at all; that it was some strange masquerader of whose identity she never could be sure again. There had been no special devotion between Helen and her father; he had been kind but careless, and she too had been careless, though affectionate enough; but the miserable pang with which she seemed to lose her hold of him, and with him of everything solid and steadfast in the world, was more terrible than anything she had ever felt before. Her life seemed to be rent up by the roots. Janey, whimpering and astonished, took refuge in her corner, and by-and-by, worn out, dropped happily asleep. But Helen could not sleep. Worn out too, but watchful, she sat upright by her father's side, not venturing to look at him, seeing the long, flat, level lines of the country fly past the carriage windows with a tedium that made her eyes ache. And he too sat bolt upright, not looking at her. She had found him out; and he perceived that she had found him out; but yet she had not got a step farther, or discovered any real clue to the meaning of the flight which she thus shared.

They travelled all that night, the second since they left home, Janey sleeping in her corner, but Helen sitting sleepless, though worn to death; and next day in the forenoon stopped at a sleepy little French town, by a slow, pale, chalk river, amid interminable lines of poplars. Words could not tell the weariness which possessed Helen, the overmastering desire she felt to lay herself down anywhere, it did not matter where; while at the same time the routine of the continued movement had got into her brain, and it seemed to have become natural to go on and on, seeing those long lines of distance, those flying plains, monotonous and endless, those rivers and fields. When the train stopped with a jar, and with cramped limbs they stepped out and stood upon the ordinary soil, the stoppage itself was a shock to Helen's nerves. It was mid-day of a bright October day when they drove over the stony pavement in a jumbling omnibus, and rattled into a large square inhabited by a cathedral and town-hall of imposing architecture, with two little soldiers in red uniforms lounging under an archway, and two people crossing the sunshine, going in different directions. The white houses, tall and trim, with their green *persiennes*, the great tower of the church cutting the blue sky, the two figures crossing the sunshine printed themselves vaguely on Helen's mind. She could not see anything plainly for that vision of her father always before her who was not her father. She did not like to look at him, yet saw his changed countenance and false beard all the time with that sense of the insupportable which only our own flesh and blood ever give us. She could not forget it as Janey forgot, from whose little mind the incident of the night had fled like last year's snow. Janey ran into the bare, carpetless room at the inn, and climbed up upon the wooden chair at the window, and called to papa— "Why do they have all the curtains drawn at the windows, and why is there nobody in the street, and why are the soldiers so little, and what have they dot red trousers for?" cried Janey. The blow had gone from her recollection. She thought no more of that novelty of the beard. She had slept all night, and she was no longer tired, though she was pale.

"Do you mean to stay here, papa?" said Helen. It is dreadful to sit at table with any one and not to speak. She could not

bear it; if he would not say anything to her, she must talk to him.

"It does not look a very interesting place, you mean? No picture galleries or fine things to see. That is a pity; but if you do not object to it too much, it suits me to stay here for a little while."

"I do not object at all, papa," said poor Helen, ready to cry, "only—only——" She looked at him with wistful eyes.

"Only what? If you don't object to me and everything about me, you should try not to look as if you did. Understand once for all, that *I* understand my own motives and you don't. And I don't mean to be forced to explain by any one, much less my own child."

"Papa," said Janey, "you shouldn't be cross. You dave me a slap last night, but I never was cross. I did not look like this," and she covered her innocent forehead with the most portentous of frowns. "I forgave you," said the child, mastering the "g" with an effort, and looking up at him with a countenance clear as the day; not like the troubled face of Helen. The man was more touched than words could say. He caught her up in his arms.

"Yes, my little darling," he said, "I did; God forgive me! I gave this dear little cheek a tap. I may have done other things as wrong, but none that I regretted so much. But you forgive your poor old father, Janey. I would not hurt you, my pet, not a hair of your pretty head, for the world."

"I knew you would be sorry, papa," said the little girl with the air of a little queen. Then she lifted up her tiny forefinger, with serious yet mischievous warning, "But you sould never be cross," she said.

How different was Helen's state from the innocent, tender play of the child! She sat immovable and looked on at this pretty scene, seeing her father's countenance change, the hard lines in it melt, a tender light come over it. He kissed his little Janey with a kind of reverential passion. "I will try, my little love," he said, as humble as a child. And while he kissed her half weeping, and she clung with both her little arms round his neck, Helen felt herself rigid as stone. She could not be touched even by that which was most pathetic in this little episode—the real emotion of the man whose conscience was certainly not void of greater offences, yet whose heart melted at the pretty majesty of his child's reproof, her innocent counsel and authority. Helen sat and looked on like some one entirely outside, a world apart from this tender union. She did not share the emotion of it, nor the sweetness. Her heart seemed made of lead ; her eyes were dry as summer dust. She turned away from them, not to see the innocent rapture of the father and child. The bare little *salle à manger*, with its long table thinly covered ; the bare boards ; the windows with their close white curtains ; the all-prevailing odour of soup and cigars ; the clashing of the ostler's pails outside ; the high-pitched voices ; the language only half comprehensible, made up a scene for her which she never forgot. Their strange meal was over—a dozen unknown dishes—and they had been left with a plate of fruit on the table and a bottle of *vin du pays*, which Helen thought so sour. She was wearied to death, but she no longer felt that devouring desire to lie down and go to sleep. The pain had roused her ; it seemed to her for the moment as if she would never sleep again.

Then she went up-stairs to the little bare bedroom above, where two white beds stood side by side, two windows with the same white closely fixed curtains, a carpetless, curtainless room, with everything as bare and wooden, as clean and white as could be desired. She had to open the new trunk and take out all their new things, which did not belong to her, which belonged to a fugitive, the daughter of a man who had fled from his own country and home in disguise, and at the dead of night. It seemed to her that she could never tolerate this livery of shame, or think of it save with a burning as of disgrace upon her countenance. Perhaps it was partly because she was so worn out that she took everything so tragically. She went out afterwards to see the town, following her father, who led little Janey by the hand, delighted by all her questions. The little girl prattled without ceasing, asking questions about everything. "Why are they such little soldiers ?" she said ; "they are like the little men in my Swiss village ; and why have they got red trousers instead of red coats ? is it with walking in the enemy's blood, papa ? like the Bible," said Janey.

"Hush, hush ! there cannot be anything like that in the Bible, Janey."

"Ah ! that is because you don't read the lessons. You should read the lessons every day," said Janey, delighted with her *rôle* of counsellor, "like Nurse, papa ! How funny it would be when Nurse went up-stairs and found only dolly in my little bed, and Janey gone away !" She laughed, and then looked at him with a look of examination more keen

than that timid, wistful look of Helen's. "But I like this," she added ; "it is funny. Why do the little children wear caps ? and what funny little shoes that make such a noise ! and why do they all speak French, papa ? Who taught them to speak French ?" Janey, in her fresh wonder, put all the threadbare questions that everybody has put before. She skipped upon the rough stones by her father's side, holding his hand tight ; and the three people who were in the great square (besides the soldiers) looked upon the pair with kindly eyes, and pointed out to each other that the newly-arrived Anglais worshipped his child. They have the domestic instinct above all—they adore their infants. "But *tiens*," they said, "is it madame the young wife who follows with a look so *maussade* ?"

The sympathies of these spectators were all with the father and the child. Helen followed like a creature in a dream. The great, silent, empty, open cathedral, with its altars all dressed in artificial lilies, and the scent of incense still in the air, came into her silent picture gallery with all its details distinct, yet strange ; and the long line of boulevard with its trees, and the white houses with their veiled windows, and the clanking of the *sabots*, and the little soldiers in the archway. They gave her no pleasure as of a novel sight, but they completed the vague, feverish world around her, so dim to her mental perception, yet keenly clear to her outward eye in the sharp blueness of the sky, the vivid tints of the south. They went over all the town thus, mounting to the ramparts, going through all the narrow streets : Janey dancing along with her father's hand in hers, Helen following, silent like a creature walking in her sleep, taking in all the novel scene only as a background to the pain of her soul.

CHAPTER IV.

THE little city of Sainte-Barbe was the quaintest and most slumbrous of little French towns, and that is saying a great deal. The walls were intact and in good order, supplying the inhabitants with pleasant walks, which few people took advantage of. Their pretence at defence was antiquated and useless, but then there was nothing to defend nor any enemy intending to attack. From the ramparts you looked out upon a great plain bounded towards the north with hills, and dropping southwards into those low swelling slopes and hillocks which form the best vineyards. Sainte-Barbe was on the edge of a rich wine country verging upon the Côte d'Or ; but there were no vineyards close to the town, which rose up, with its cluster of towers, its high walls, and peaked roofs, out of the plain. It is to be supposed that in former days it had been a centre of more important life, for the cathedral was large enough for a metropolis, and the great town-hall, with its fine belfry, looked like one of the warlike municipalities of the Middle Ages. These two great buildings stood and sunned themselves, resting from whatever labours they might once have known, in a sort of dull beatitude—the one with half-a-dozen erratic worshippers coming and going, the other with three little red-legged sol-diers under its grand gateway. Now and then a tourist who had heard of these build-ings stopped for a few hours on his way from Italy to Paris to see them ; but the fame of them was fast fading out, now that nobody thinks of posting from Paris to Dijon, and it was the rarest thing in the world to see a stranger in the streets. For the first week the townsfolk said among themselves, "Tiens l voilà les Anglais " when Mr. Goul-burn and his daughters appeared ; but at the end of that time became familiar with the appearance of them. It was a curious life which they led at the Lion d'Or—in a quaint discomfort, which may be amusing to tourists in high spirits, but to the timid and troubled English girl was the strangest travesty of existence. The mixture of small discomforts with great troubles is perhaps the combina-tion above all others which procures entire and complete confusion in life. And the want of a room to sit in other than that wooden bedroom, where every movement of a chair jarred upon the bare planks, began after a while to mingle in Helen's mind with all the painful circumstances of their flight, so that she scarcely knew what it was that made her so wretched, so disjoined from all her past. Twice a day the little party ate in company with some of the best people in Sainte-Barbe. M. le Notaire, who was un-married, an old bachelor, and M. le Maire, who was a widower, took their meals regu-larly at the Lion d'Or. They tied their napkins round their bottle of wine when they left after one meal, and tucked them under their chins when they next sat down. On Sunday there was an officer who came in his uniform, with his sword clanking, who im-pressed Janey with great awe, accompanied by his wife and their little boy and bonne who sat down next her charge and dined too, cutting the child's meat for him, and having a little wine poured out for her by

her mistress from the family bottle. Janey could not eat her own dinner, so absorbed was she in watching this party. She pulled Helen's dress to call her attention a dozen times in a minute. " Oh, what would Nurse say ? " she cried, with big eyes of astonish-ment. " Look, Helen, he has some of that that you would not let me have, and he is so little—much more little than me. And he has got wine : and oh, look ! he has put his knife in his mouth—he will kill himself. And now he has his hand in, the nasty little boy ! "

" Cela amuse Mademoiselle de voir manger mon petit," said the lady across the table in a tone of offence.

Helen blushed as if she had been caught in a mortal sin. " Oh no, Madame—only—elle ne sait pas——" she murmured in apology.

" He has dot his knife in his mouth, and that will kill him," said Janey. " She ought to tell him. Oh, little boy, little boy, *couteau— bouche !* " she cried, with the anxiety of her age to put everything right.

Mr. Goulburn tried to apologise. " My little girl thinks it is her business to set every-body right. She takes it upon her to regulate my conduct and manners. I hope you will forgive the little impertinent. Besides, she is astonished to see the *bonne* by your side, Madame, at table. It is contrary to our English usage. Forgive her," he said.

" Oh, rien, Monsieur," said the French lady politely. " We all know that England is the most aristocratic of countries. Do not apologise ; there is great good in that—the *canaille* are kept in their place."

" The *canaille* are in all places, Madame," said M. le Maire. " They are among us when we least suspect it. Persons of the best manners, the most irreproachable in appear-ance——"

" Ah, if M. le Maire takes the point of view of the highest morals ! It is well known that the blessed Apostles were but fishermen and labourers," said the lady ; " but we could not now invite a sailor smelling of the sea, or a ploughman fresh from the fields, to eat with us. There are lines of demarcation."

" Madame," said the Maire, " I have been warned from the police of a person com-pletely *comme il faut*, handsome, young, tall, well brought up, a hero of romance — you would be enchanted with his description— who has done everything that a man can do of perfidious and wicked—if he should pay us a visit here——"

" Ah, monsieur, what a dreadful idea ! But perhaps it is evil companions, bad in·

fluences—and then, when one is young, everything may be recovered."

"With *le beau sexe* youth is always the first of virtues," said the Notaire.

"Listen—they are not always young—Madame should have seen the journals of England a little time ago—Monsieur here could tell us, no doubt. A great company of merchants in London has lately made bankruptcy. Impossible to tell you what ruin they have produced. The great, the small, widows and orphans, poor officers in retreat, little functionaries, priests—what in England they call clergymen—all ruined, without a penny, without bread!" said the Maire, throwing up his hands. "Mon Dieu! even to hear of it makes one suffer. And figure to yourself the chief—he who was first in this *compagnie*, a man rich as the Indies, living *en prince*, and for whom nothing was too good, has taken flight, instead of ending his life with a pistol-shot, as would have been done in France—has taken flight, with enormously of money in his pockets. You have seen it, perhaps, in the journals. Such things happen only in England. Mon Dieu! he has saved himself with the money of others. And one talks of *canaille!*" the Maire concluded, wiping his forehead. He was warm with indignation, feeling the force of his own eloquence.

Helen did not understand all this—or nearly all; but she caught a word now and then, and her father's face filled her with alarm. It had been smiling enough at first, though with that drawn and artificial smile which she had only remarked of late; but by degrees Mr. Goulburn's head had dropped, he stooped over his plate, fixing his attention on that, yet now and then directed a furtive glance from under his eyebrows at the speaker. And his face grew ghastly pale, yet he took out his handkerchief and wiped his forehead with it. His hands trembled as he raised his glass to his lips. The *vin du pays* was not likely to inspire much courage, but he drank a large quantity, large enough to make the Maire and the Notary stare. All this Helen remarked, though perhaps no one else did. He did everything he could to preserve appearances; but her attention was roused, and she was on the alert and saw everything, and almost more than everything. What had he to do with this story of disgrace and ruin? Some one came in at this moment, a stranger, who was placed in a seat on her other hand; but she was so intent upon her father that she did not even see who it was. There was a pause, which

seemed terrible to her—and to him; but which to the others was a most natural and simple, nay, flattering moment of silence after the Maire's impressive remarks.

"You say such things happen only in England; is no one ever bankrupt in France?" Mr. Goulburn said at last.

"Alas!" said M. le Maire, "misfortune comes in all countries. But a French *commerçant* bears it—not so well as your countrymen, Monsieur. I have known men who have undergone that and now hold up their heads again; and I have known men, *ma foi!* who could not bear it, who thought of nothing but a pistol-shot. One follows the customs of one's country. I have heard that Englishmen grow fat upon it. Pardon, you understand that is a pleasantry. No one can have more respect for the English than I."

"It is a pleasantry, M. le Maire, which an Englishman hears with very little pleasure," said Mr. Goulburn. Helen, looking at him with her anxious eyes, felt that her father was glad of some cause for seeming angry, and caught at this justification of his own excitement. But while her mind was intent upon him, watching him with an eager anxiety and curiosity beyond words, she started to hear herself addressed on the other side. "Is it possible that it is Miss Goulburn? Can I be mistaken?" a pleasant voice said in English. She turned round quickly, and found a fair-haired and very sun-burnt young man, whom she did not at first recognise, and upon whom she looked with suspicion and alarm. Her fears had been excited, she could scarcely tell how or why. Every one who knew her seemed a possible enemy. Were they not fugitives, whatever might be the cause?

"You do not remember me," said the newcomer; "which, perhaps, is not wonderful. I left Fareham four years ago, Miss Goulburn; but I think I cannot be mistaken in you. You were only a child then—and now! but still I think it is you: and perhaps you remember my name, Charley Ashton? I went to India——"

"Yes, I recollect. Are you going home now to—to Fareham?" Helen said, with fright in her eyes.

"That we should meet here of all places in the world! Yes, I am on my way home; and there is all about the cathedral in Murray, and besides there is a bit of engineering I wanted to see, and I had a day to spare—what a lucky chance for me! You, I suppose, are making the grand tour, as it used to be called. Travelling, like necessity, makes one acquainted with strange quarters. This is not much like Fareham, is it?" he said, with a laugh. That careless, happy laugh, without thought of evil! Helen looked at him, admiring it as an old man might have done.

"No; we are only here—for a little while."

She knew by instinct that this would be their last night at Sainte-Barbe, and that she must not encourage any renewal of acquaintance. The young man looked at her with such a look of kindly inquiry, almost tender in the sympathy that mingled with it, that Helen felt the tears come to her eyes. He divined that there was something to be sorry for, and he was ready to be sorry and to sympathize, whatever the trouble might be—though the troubles, he said to himself with a smile, of the rich man's daughter were not likely to be very hard to bear.

"That is like my luck," he said; "unless you are going back to England, which would be the best of all. Then I should ask leave to follow in your wake. There is no one now to care much when I get home; a day or two sooner or later doesn't matter. My mother is not there now to mind. And to tell the truth, Miss Goulburn," said young Ashton, "I am just as glad to put off the first plunge. Poor old father! I dare say he'll be glad to see me; but to find *her* not only gone, but with another in her place!"

"Poor Mr. Ashton was so lonely," said Helen, coming out of her own troubles for one moment, "and Miss Temple is so kind: it does you good to speak to her. She never meant any harm. She was so sorry for him —do not be angry with Miss Temple. I think I love her," the girl said, the tears slowly gathering in her eyes, "better—oh, yes, a great deal better than any one—than any other woman in the world."

"Do you?" he said, touched by the sight. Charley Ashton did not know how many other troubles in poor Helen's heart found grateful outlet in those tears. They dropped upon her dress and frightened her lest any one else should see them, but the young man was altogether melted by Helen's emotion. "That shall be my best reason for loving— at least for liking her too," he said. "Thank you for showing me how much you care for her. What a lucky inspiration I had to come to Sainte-Barbe! I had been just thinking of you, wondering if you would be much changed—if, perhaps, I should find you at Fareham."

"I think I am very much changed," she said, sadly shaking her head—while he looked at her, smiling with a look of subdued yet tender admiration. He did not venture to look all he felt, yet he could not keep it from appearing.

"Yes, I think you are changed," he said, with a confused laugh. She was thinking of the last week, he of the last five years. He had admired her then as a child—for Helen had been tall and precocious. Now he could not tell her how much more he admired her as a woman, and Helen was too sadly preoccupied to interpret justly the lingering glance that dwelt upon her. She had never had any lover, nor was she at all aware that the Vicar's son had any special recollection of her; that he should recognise her at all filled her with surprise. But at the same time the sense of something sympathetic by her side, of some one who was young like herself, and English, and looked kindly at her, gave the girl a sense of consolation. He laughed, but certainly he meant nothing unkind. The moment after young Ashton gave Helen, all unawares, a sudden blow which forced her back upon herself. He said with a little eagerness, but calmly, as if it were the most ordinary question in the world. "Do you go back soon to Fareham? I have come home on sick leave. I shall have only a little while at home. I hope I shall see you while I am there."

"Oh!" said Helen, trembling all over with the shock, "I do not know—Papa has never told me. Perhaps—we may not be back for a long time; perhaps—not at all. I don't know."

"Not back at all! Has Mr. Goulburn sold it?" young Ashton said, and his changed countenance grew long. He was as much disappointed as she was startled; and for a moment both looked, though from very different reasons, as though not at all indisposed to mingle their tears.

"I don't know," said Helen. She looked away from him, her voice shook, there was trouble indescribable in her face. And he remembered that he had been gone for four years; that he had not heard very much about them for some time back; that many changes might happen, especially in the fortunes of a man in business, however great he might be, and apparently beyond the assaults of fortune. What could young Ashton say, or do, to show his sympathy? He did not even know how far he might inquire.

"I beg your pardon," he said. Helen looked up at him timidly, and gave him a little nod of assent, and a faint smile. She granted him his pardon freely. She thanked him for the feeling in his face, but she said nothing more. The secret was not hers, and she did not even know what the secret was. Meanwhile her father had begun to see what was going on. He had looked furtively from the corner of his eyes at the stranger, and had ended by remembering who he was; and he did not know what young Ashton knew, where he had come from, what he might be doing there. When he saw that Helen was fully engaged in conversation, he got up softly and walked away. The sight of a face he had once known made his heart beat wildly, and filled him with a sickening sensation. He went out by a door behind, so as never to come within the stranger's range of vision. What did he want here? and what would the girl tell him? Would she have the sense to hold her tongue? though, indeed, the very sight of her would be enough if young Ashton knew. He began, without a moment's delay, to put back his clothes into his portmanteau, and prepare again for flight. Who would have thought that such a thing could happen here? Had the danger been greater, he would have understood. For the sudden appearance of pursuers in search of him, he was always prepared; but not for the ludicrous simplicity of a peril like this; a neighbour's son! What evil genius had brought him here? It seemed a very long time before Helen came up-stairs. It had relieved her to see her father disappear, and she had yielded to the pleasure of talking to her contemporary, her old friend (as she thought). But after all, in about ten minutes she had held out her hand to him timidly, rising up as she did so, to go away. "But I shall see you to-morrow?" he said. She only smiled faintly and said, "Perhaps," but even as she said so shook her head. In her heart she felt certain that they would leave Sainte-Barbe that night.

And so they did. In France all the great trains go by night; there was one very late which called at Sainte-Barbe, on the way to Paris. The clatter and clang of the omnibus which met this train disturbed the whole town at midnight so much, that M. le Maire had set every kind of machinery in motion to have it discontinued; but as the convenience of the two extremities of the railway, Marseilles and Paris, forbade this, the authorities paid no attention to the protest of Sainte-Barbe. The few guests in the Lion d'Or felt a double grievance this night, in that the omnibus, after making its usual noisy circuit from the stables, waited, pawing and champ-

ing for five minutes, under the *porte cochère*, having baggage placed upon it, and carrying away travellers at that hour. Who could they be? Oh, *les Anglais:* that went without saying. Certainly *les Anglais;* they were the sort of people who would do such a thing simply because it was unlike the rest of the world—though it was the action of a fiend, the landlady exclaimed afterwards, to take such an infant from her rest at such an hour. Young Ashton was still astir, smoking his cigar out of the window with a quite unnecessary regard for the feelings of his hosts, when the omnibus turned out of the great doorway. He thought he saw a pale face look up at his window in the uncertain glimmer of the moon, which was dim with flying clouds, and he let his cigar drop on the head of an ostler below in consternation. Could it be that they had gone away? "Gone away because I am here!" this young man said to himself. But it seemed a thing too impossible to be true.

CHAPTER V.

IT was scarcely daylight of the ruddy but chill October morning, when the travellers set out from the station at which they had been dropped. They had been left there to wait for the diligence, which only left on the arrival of another train from Paris. All had been black and silent at the little station of Montdard, when they were shot out, to the dismay of two or three half-awakened officials, who regarded them with alarm and suspicion. It was very rarely indeed that any one arrived in the middle of the night at Montdard, except from Paris, the train from which did not come in till five o'clock. What were they to do in the meantime? Mr. Goulburn had got little Janey in his arms fast asleep. With her dangling feet, and her pale little head thrown back on his shoulder, she looked more like a sick young woman, long and wasted, than a child. Helen followed closely as a shadow, asking no questions, following every indication of her father's will, silent and watchful, cold and miserable. The gloom around and the suspicious looks of the railway men, and the cold that went to her heart, all began to be familiar. It did not even occur to her to think of the existence which had ended about ten days ago, the life of warmth and luxury and softness, which knew no disturbance, which was waited upon by assiduous servants, and spent in such careful guardianship. She thought of it no more. What she wished for was not her draped and curtained room at Fareham, with its carpets in which the feet sank, but a comfortable bench somewhere, or rush-bottomed chair in a corner out of the wind, where she could get her ulster more closely about her, and put a shawl over Janey's feet; or, as the very climax of comfort, another white-curtained wooden room with two little beds, where she could lie down with Janey next to her. Helen in her heart had bidden farewell to Fareham for ever and ever. She did not know even where they were going, and it gave her a gleam of comfort to hear her father explain to the sleepy yet vigilant porter in his blouse, that he was going to Latour, where there was to be a sale of the woods on the property of the late Count Bernard de Vieux-bois. Mr. Goulburn explained that he had heard of this only at the last moment, and that as he had no time to lose, he had been obliged to bring his daughters with him, though the journey was so fatiguing for the little one. The French heart is very open to children, and the man with the blouse managed to open the door of a dismal *salle*, where at least *la petite* would be sheltered from the cold wind. How kind they are to Janey, Helen thought. The rough peasant-porter with his bristly beard, a man who might have figured in a revolutionary riot, and probably had done so, one time or another, caressed a floating lock of her fair hair which fell from her father's shoulder with his rough hand, with the softest look of reverence and pity, "Pauvre petite!"—he brought an old braided overcoat, fine, but faded, from an inner room to lay on her feet. "It would have been better to leave her *à la maison*," he said. "A la maison!" People who know no better, say the French have no word that means home; but Helen felt this word go through and through her like a sword. Where was the house to which Janey belonged, where she could find her little bed and her little corner by right? As for Mr. Goulburn he put himself on the bench against the wall in the most painfully constrained attitude to make Janey comfort-able. His face, as he looked down upon the child, was lighted up with the most trembling tenderness. He had wronged many people and deprived many children of bread, but he loved his own with a pas-sionate devotion. He could not separate himself from his child. Helen, so watchful beside him, saw it all with an ache of wonder in her heart. She did not understand, per-haps, that clinging of a guilty man to the one thing innocent and sweet in his life. She was sorry for her poor little sister thus dragged about the world, and perhaps a little sorry for herself. If it was necessary for him to fly from one place to another, why should little Janey be made to fly too? And Helen turned her thoughts back upon the Lion d'Or with unspeakable regret. It was not an attractive place, but still it was shelter and safety. What thoughts were going on in her father's mind, who could say? There were other places of refuge which would have been safer than France, but he had little time to choose. It was not much more than chance which had determined the route they took in leaving England, and he had remembered Sainte-Barbe as the most unfrequented place he had ever seen. But the village which he had chosen must surely be out of the world if ever village was. Among the hills of Burgundy, above the vineyards, beyond the reach of commerce, in the country where the old Gauls fought, and where even the Prussians had not penetrated —what could be more safe? and yet who could guarantee its safety? "We should have been better in Spain," he was saying to himself.

The diligence started at five o'clock for Latour. It was speedily filled, in the little interior, with five or six young peasant women, in their white caps, each with a baby, little foundlings, or the children of poor shopkeepers and workpeople in Paris, brought to the country to be reared—the healthy hills of *la Haute Bourgogne* being much approved for that purpose. The travellers managed with great difficulty to get possession for themselves of the *banquette*, a covered seat like a sort of phaeton, with leathern curtains capable of closing in front, which occupies the place behind the coachman in these rural vehicles. They had ten long leagues to traverse before they got to their journey's end. Poor little Janey, very pale and shivering, lost for the first time her childish adaptability, and whimpered piti-fully, with cold feet, and the wretchedness of her disturbed rest; and a more melancholy and jaded party never confronted the morn-ing mists. They rattled along as in a dream, seeing the country gradually unfold itself, now just visible in the faint grey of the dawn, anon developing into clearer light, the hills rising black against the yellow east, then showing their grass slopes and broken bits of cliff as the sun struck here and there a long golden dart driving away the shadows. A crisp sprinkling of hoar frost was upon the fields, and the roads were hard, and resounded under the horses' feet, which made sound enough, with all the jingling of the rude harness, and all the creaking of the springless coach, for a whole cavalcade. In front of the *banquette*, beside the coachman, sat a large priest and a man wrapped in the thick blue overcoat with its braided collar which the French peasant loves. The talk of these two was all of the old Count de Vieux-bois's

woods. The hills between which the road passed were entirely bare of trees, and Count Bernard had been the subject of much pleasantry, the priest said, when he planted his lands with an unprofitable crop of forest. But time had proved Count Bernard to be right. These voices went on dreamily in Helen's ear, making a sort of drowsy song to

the accompaniment of the wheels and the horses' hoofs. But Mr. Goulburn listened closely to all the heavy talk. The impulse of trade was strong in him, and the idea of turning over money now in his present downfall and fugitive condition roused him. He had seized upon the pretext, catching it up at the moment of necessity from an advertisement in one of the papers, to give an excuse for his hurried journey. But the idea pleased him the more he dwelt upon it. He listened with the greatest attention to all that was being said; he recovered the activity and energy of mind that was natural to him. To outwit fate in such a way would be in itself a kind of triumph. He did not disturb little Janey's head, which lay on his shoulder, but he withdrew his arm from her as his thoughts quickened. A man of business is always a man of business, however direful may be the plight in which he finds himself. Pale, un-

cared-for, haggard as he looked in the morning light, his bosom's lord sat more lightly upon its throne than it had done since he left England. So far even as appearances went, there was this good in Mr. Goulburn's false decorations of hair, that they did not grow in the night.

They passed through a number of villages, changing horses with much noise and clangour here and there—a proceeding which cheered up Janey almost as much as the thoughts of a bargain did her father; and through one quaint and wonderful town, all walled and embattled, where the lanterns still hung across the streets as in the days when aristocrats were hanged by that easy method of getting rid of an undesirable intruder; and by dreary old châteaux, grey and homely, without any softening of trees or park to link them to the surrounding country. By-and-by, after a long, long

2

waste of road, they came upon the masses of trees which had hung upon the horizon like clouds, and which showed where Count Vieux-bois' estates began. Beautiful feathery larches, big pines, and sturdy oaks clothed the slopes, and changed the whole character of the country. And after a while the diligence rattled into a long village street with a church at one end and a quaint old castle at the other, more imposing than anything they had yet seen. The street was irregular, now broad, now narrow, widening out in the centre into a kind of place or square, in which there were two or three white houses, several stories high, with green *persiennes* half closed. The rest of the place consisted of cottages, mostly thatched and humble, with a little post-office, and a cavernous shop in which were all kinds of possible and impossible goods. The "general merchant" of France is different from him of England, just as sabots and blouses are different from country-made shoes and fustian coats. And at Latour the sabots and the blouses were universal. M. le Curé himself wore a pair over his shoes in bad weather, leaving them at the door of every house he visited. The diligence stopped with a jarring shock and noise, suddenly drawn up before the humble door of another Lion d'Or, a popular sign in the district. But this one was little more than an *auberge*, a village public-house, with its description posted up in straggling letters, *ICI on loge à Pied et à CHEVAL.* There was no *porte-cochère*, no courtyard to mark the importance of the hotel, but only a *salle à manger* looking out upon the pavement, low-roofed and dark, and smelling as usual, but worse than usual, of bad cigars and the *pot-au-feu*. There were several men seated at the long table eating their breakfast when Helen and little Janey followed their father into the room; one or two others who had · finished their meal were smoking their cigars—they were all talking in high voices, harsh to unaccustomed ears. The farther end, the only unoccupied place, was far from the window, and in a kind of twilight. Little Janey grasped her father's hand tight till the little soft fingers almost hurt him. "Oh, take me away," she cried, "take me away. I won't do there. Take me home, papa—take me to my own home." He took her in his arms and carried her to the quiet corner. "My little pet," he said, "I wish I could; but it's a long, long way off, Janey. You must try and be contented here." "Oh, papa," said the child, "I want to

do home. I want to do home! I don't like it here. I don't like—nothing at all but —home." "Janey, Janey!—speak to her, Helen. You will like it better after—the people are always very kind to you. And you are tired, my little love. You will like it better when you know——" "I want to do home!" cried Janey; but the sudden odour of the soup put under her nose wrought a revolution in her mind. "And I am so hungry," she said, her tears drying up. She raised her head from her father's shoulder where she had been past all consolation the moment before—and slid down from his knee. Ah! why is six so much more easy to console than eighteen? or eighteen than fifty? might be said in other circumstances. But in the present case the father and the little child had both regained their spirits, and it was only Helen whose heart lay like a lump of lead in her breast. That evening Mr. Goulburn called her into the small room which he was to occupy, with an air of some embarrassment. There had been no sitting-room possible at Sainte-Barbe, yet it was practicable to occupy a corner in the *salle à manger*, when all was quiet there. But in the Lion d'Or at Latour it was never quiet. In the evening the villagers came in to consume slowly their sour *piquette*, or bitter *chope*, and fill the place with clouds of smoke; and the two crowded yet scantily furnished bedrooms, in which the strangers were lodged, were the only places in which they could talk. Mr. Goulburn called Helen into his room. He was embarrassed and did not know how to begin. Helen's look of inquiry seemed to paralyze him. He stammered and hesitated and cleared his throat. At length he said, with the rapidity of one who is anxious to get over a painful operation, "I wanted to speak to you, Helen. There is one little matter—unnecessary to enter into my reasons for it. While we are here, I mean to call myself by my mother's name, Harford, instead of Goulburn." "Papa!" her pale countenance was suffused with the most violent colour. Pale, worn-out, and weary as her looks had been a moment since, she was of the colour of passion now. "I mean what I say," he said sharply, his own disguised face catching fire at hers. There was a touch of shame in his anger, yet his eyes blazed into a sudden burst of fury, which again was partly put on to hide the shame. "I do not see that I need enter into all my reasons to you. I am satisfied that it is expedient, or I would not do it; and that ought to be enough for my child."

"It is not enough, it is not enough, papa," said Helen. "I cannot call myself out of my name."

"Then you will do what you please," he said; "but I shall employ the name I have told you; you can do what you please: but in that case you shall not be owned as a daughter of mine."

The world seemed to go round and round with Helen, the poor little world so bare and poverty-stricken, the walls with their blue and white striped paper, the bare boards and white-curtained windows. She looked at him piteously, seeing his face blurred and magnified through the two tears of pain and passion in her eyes. "Why is it?" she said with a pathetic appeal; "oh, tell me why it is! If I knew why, perhaps I could bear it better. Oh, papa, tell me why!"

His first impulse was to silence her imperiously and send her away, but a better inspiration followed. "Did you never hear of men in business who were ruined, Helen? Did you never read of destruction coming in a single day? I was a rich man a fortnight since, and never dreamt that such a calamity—was possible. It came upon me all at once. Misfortune of the most complete kind—ruin. I had nothing for it but to take you and the child and hurry away."

"Oh, is that all, papa? are you sure that is all. Not—what they were speaking of last night?—not—oh, forgive me!—I did not understand; only the loss of your money—no more than that, papa?"

A painful contraction, almost a grimace, went over his face. The rage which he had partially assumed before was now real, but he did not show it. He clenched his fist at her, but kept it in his pocket, and put on a smile which looked something between a grin and a snarl. "Most people would think it was quite enough—and more than enough. Now you know my secret. I did not want—to make you unhappy," he said.

"Oh, unhappy! it is the contrary; if you knew how happy you have made me!" said Helen, with the first real smile that had visited them for days in her wet eyes. "You have taken off the weight *here*—oh, it is all gone, and I can breathe. You have lost your money, poor papa! I am so sorry and yet I can't help being glad. After all, what does it matter? We have enough, and we are together. Oh, if you knew the things that have been going through my wicked, wretched heart—

papa, will you forgive me?" the girl cried, growing pale and clasping her hands. "Oh, I ought to ask your pardon on my knees!"

"We will dispense with that formula," said her father, with a chilly smile which froze her fervour; "perhaps this will teach you to refrain from hasty judgment. There can scarcely be a case, let me entreat you to believe, in which I shall not be the best judge of us two."

"Yes, papa," she said submissively: then added with a timid look, "but would it not have been better to have stayed, and met it in the face, whatever it was? To be unfortunate is not any harm. What could ruin do to us, but to make us poor? Papa——"

A sharp laugh from him cut her short; he could have struck her as he struck Janey when she found out his disguise, but he did not dare to treat the elder sister so, and she was more easily managed in the other way. "It seems to me," he said, "that you are doing precisely what you have just promised not to do. We have agreed that I am the best judge, and the judge I mean to be, in my own concerns. Therefore go to bed, and recollect that to-morrow you are Miss Harford—and know nothing about that other name."

She shrank a little away, looking at him with piteous eyes. "Yes, papa," she said; "but——" and stood looking with a beseeching, tender entreaty. She clasped her hands, but she did not say anything, though every moving line of her face, the glimmer of moisture in her eyes, the quiver in her lips, all spoke. In his impatience he stamped his foot on the floor.

"By Jove, you will drive me mad!" he cried, "with your fancies and your hesitations. Do what I tell you—hold your tongue if you are so scrupulous about an innocent social pretence. What does it matter to those French clowns what name I call myself by? Will they be any the wiser? And I hold that a man has as much right to his mother's name as his father's. It is the same thing. There, Helen, I forgive your nonsense, because you are tired out, poor child! go to bed."

"Yes, papa," she said, but still she did not budge. All this time the voices and noises were going on below, sounds of disputation, quick fire of talk, more vivacious and louder in tone than anything English; outside and in, there were sounds of conversation going on. All this Babel of sound continued while these two quiet English persons had their explanation, which meant so much; the rest meant nothing. When Helen thought of it after, she always remembered the discussion in the *salle à manger*, and the clatter of words which Jeannette on the top story flung down to her mistress below-stairs.

But as for herself she had said her say. Her father bade her good night in a peremptory tone, dismissing her beyond appeal. But he was very kind, and kissed her, though she was conscious of a thrill and tremor about him when he did so, which she could not understand to be suppressed rage. But as it was, Helen retired with a weight gone from her heart, as she said—yet not such a complete relief as she had felt at the first moment. Only ruin, only poverty! these were nothing. But then—people were sorry for men who had lost all their money, nobody was cruel to them, or thought it their fault; it was nothing to be ashamed of; the best people in the world (she reflected) have been poor; therefore why, *why* had he fled from home? why had he not faced the worst? Better even, Helen thought, to have endured a little vexation, to have given up everything, than to have become a fugitive, and worn disguises, and feared a friendly face, and changed their name. The weight came back as these strange details recurred to her mind. That false beard! would any deprivation, any scorn of cruel creditors, any misfortune have been so bad, so debasing, so shameful as *that?* And why should Charley Ashton's honest face have so appalled him? Ah! Charley Ashton could meet the gaze of all the world and never flinch; he would not disguise himself, nor hide himself, whatever might be the danger. Helen tried to represent to herself that she was not the judge, that her father must know best; but there is nothing so difficult to believe as this, especially when reason seems all on our side.

The pain was gnawing again when she lay down by Janey's side. Poverty: but we are not poor! Helen said to herself, almost leaping up in her bed. They had spent a great deal of money and spared nothing; indeed, there had never been any attempt to spare anything. It was not an art they understood. But, happily, sleep began to steal upon her young eyes, even in the midst of her agitation. The night before had been one long vigil; she could not be kept awake, even by the misery of these thoughts.

CHAPTER VI.

NEXT morning Latour was more cheerful than usual. The men who had come to inspect the woods were not indeed picturesque figures, nor of a very elevated class, but still they made the village street lively, which was delightful to Janey, and cheered Helen in spite of herself. Everything looks a little more cheerful, more comfortable, in the morning. The sun shone down the village street, catching here and there upon a little window in a thatched roof, upon the weathercock on the tower of the château, and on the church spire—and shedding a ruddy glow, touched with frost, over all the country. The woods looked as if they had been crimsoned permanently by the red tint in the sunshine, so harmonious were their hues. The road was flecked by yellow bars looking like rays of gold; everything was mellow and warm in colour, notwithstanding the chill of coming winter in the air. Little groups of men took their way in a broken stream towards the woods. Some of them burly French farmers, of the better sort, with close-cropped heads, and overcoats of picturesque green-blue, that favoured tint which is "the fashion;" some in blouses, not so ambitious; with one or two wood merchants from the neighbouring towns, prim and well-shaven, in the frock-coat of respectability. There had been a great deal of drinking and bargaining in all the *cabarets* about, the evening before. The villagers had given their advice, especially those among them who were the least creditable members of society, the poachers of the commune, who knew every tree. Some of them, the idlest, the least satisfactory of all, to whom the loss of a day's work was rather a pleasure than a misfortune, accompanied the intending purchasers to the woods.

"Keep up by the pond, Monsieur," said one of these fellows, attaching himself to Mr. Goulburn. "There is some oak that might build ships of war——"

"The best trees are on the Côte du Midi," said another. "If Monsieur will confide himself to me——"

"I don't mean to confide myself to any one, my good fellow," Mr. Goulburn said. He walked along a little in advance of the two, with an air alert and vigorous, restored by the new possibility of traffic.

Janey ran by her father's side, clinging to his finger, and chattering all the way. "What are they saying, papa? They speak so funny. Why don't they speak English? Couldn't they speak English if they liked?"

Mr. Goulburn was a man who liked to be popular. He was of the class which servants declare to be "not the least proud." "My little girl thinks you could speak English if you liked," he said, turning to Antoine, the most noted poacher in the district.

"Ah! je voudrais bien! I should then have the pleasure of talking to these demoiselles," the man said, taking off his hat.

"I don't like him," said little Janey. "He has a big cut on his head; he has eyes like the ogre in 'Jack the Giant-killer.' What does he want with you, papa? He will take you into a cave, and he will eat you up. I like the other one best."

The other was Baptiste, who was the son of the landlady at the Lion d'Or. It was he who advised the Côte du Midi. He knew all the coverts as well as the partridges did, or the old wolf that lurked in the darkest shades of the forest. And his woodland likings had brought him woe; but he was bent upon defending *l'Anglais*, who was his private property for the moment, his mother's lodger, from the clutches of Antoine.

When they came as far as the château, Janey consented to give up her father's finger, and to withdraw from the procession of the wood merchants. The château was not one of those deserted grey houses they had passed on their way from Montdard, but a fine mediæval building surrounded by a moat, and modernised under Louis Quatorze. It occupied three sides of a square, and at the end nearest the village was distinguished by a noble tower, covered with a pointed roof, from the windows of which the lights always shone at night, like a sort of lighthouse to the village. Helen stopped to look at it with a little quickening of natural interest. There was nothing about it of the luxury of the English house. It stood close to the road, no privacy of exquisite lawns or wealthy foliage withdrawing it from the humblest of its neighbours, a poor little plot of shrubs occupying the centre of the square within the gravelled drive. The long row of large white windows, very close to each other, which ran round two sides of the square, were undraped and unornamented, not a curtain, not a piece of furniture, showing from the outside. The great door underneath them stood open, and showed only a narrow corridor, and a bare stone staircase, mounting between two white walls. Helen stood and looked at it wistfully. She scarcely seemed to remember her own past life—yet it was a life which had no sort of connection with the cottages of Latour, the women in their white caps, the strange existence of the Lion d'Or; but here there was a kind of link of connection. If there were girls in the château, theirs might be a French version of her old life. They would be in the neighbourhood, in the village, something like what she had been. If they but knew! "But, I hope," she said to herself with a sigh, realising vividly the imagination that had presented itself to her, as if the fancied daughters of this house were certainly existing, "I hope that nothing will ever happen to *them!*" As the thought passed through her mind, the very creatures of her fancy appeared at the open door, two girls, she thought about her own age, though they were both older than Helen, dressed in the gloomy mourning of France, without an edge of white anywhere. They came out with a little clamour of talk, their voices louder than Helen was used to, though finely modulated and sweetly toned. Their French gave her that sense of giddiness, as if her head was turning round, which a new language imperfectly understood is apt to give. She went on, thinking it rude to stand and stare after they appeared; but the attraction was strong, and she turned when they had gone a few steps farther, to go back again, almost meeting the two girls as they came out of the gate. Their pleasant voices seemed to make a difference in the air. When they perceived her their lively talk broke off suddenly. Helen felt sure they were asking each other in undertones, "Who is that? Where has she come from? Do you think she looks nice?" though all in their French. She scarcely liked to look at them, but her heart beat; for they seemed to make a pause and consult each other. She wondered would they speak to her? It went to her heart when after that consultation they went on, though with a momentary hesitation. "They do not like the looks of us, Janey," she said.

"Where are they doing to?" said Janey. "What are they thinking about? I wonder if there are any little children in that big funny castle. Little children are everywhere," said the little girl mournfully, "but you tan't play with them. Helen, don't you want to do home?"

"I don't know; perhaps it would not be home now, not like what it used to be. But you are too little," said Helen with a sigh; "if I were to tell you, you wouldn't understand."

"I understand more better than you," said Janey promptly, "for papa tells me everything. I know," she said, clapping her hands, "I am not to be called the old name any more. I am little Janey Harford. Papa told me so. It is because of naughty, wicked men. Is it not funny, Helen? And you are Helen Harford too. I sing it to myself,

over and over, not to forget. Nursey wouldn't know who we were, if she were to hear. We are all different people now. Dolly that I put in my little bed is me, and I'm little Janey Harford." The child made a little chant of it as she frisked along the road. "I am little Janey Harford, I am little Janey Haar-ford!" It was a piece of delightful fun to Janey. What child can resist the pleasure of being not me, but somebody else? The spirit of an adventurer was in the little girl. She did not cling to the superstitions of propriety and a honest life as Helen did. The mystification charmed her. "It will not be you and me, but it will be two other girls," Janey said. Perhaps the profound gravity of this new step was lessened to Helen also by its effect upon her little sister. "It is I who am silly," poor Helen said to herself. She reminded herself how common it was for people to travel *incognito*. "That means out of their right name. The Queen does it!" Helen said suddenly to herself, with a sense of relief and consolation unspeakable. She knew that august lady could do no wrong.

They went back slowly through the village, following at a long interval the young ladies from the château, in whom Helen felt so great an interest, and who stopped to speak to M. le Curé, and turned round, plainly indicating to him the two figures in the distance. M. le Curé looked very closely at Helen and Janey when he passed them a little afterwards. He was an active, spare, tall man, in his long black *soutane* and his three-cornered hat of fluffy beaver on his head. He let his eyes rest with a lingering look of pleasure and interest upon the child. Most likely he took Helen, who looked older than her eighteen years, for a young mother with her child, and the Curé knew how to win the hearts of parents. Now that all the intending purchasers had passed, there were very few people about. The cottages did not stand open, as at Fareham; here and there a woman washing her vegetables outside the door, or chopping her wood into small pieces, would break the monotony, but there was no lively coming and going of gossips and neighbours. At one of the two larger houses an old man had come out, and was standing at the door. He had a handkerchief tied round his head, and a long coat, half a dressing-gown, folded across his long legs, and was looking out with the keenest malignant eyes, as if in search of some one. The Curé passed this personage with a stiff nod, but the other only grinned in reply. He grinned also at the young strangers as they came along, and at a lady who suddenly appeared from the door of the other house, dressed in the simple morning dress, fitting the figure behind, but falling straight and loose in front, which is common in France. There was a little conversation between these two, in the high-pitched voices which made every word audible.

"Madame goes out early," said the old man. " M. le Précepteur perhaps has gone to the forest to lay in wood for the winter?"

"No, Monsieur le Précepteur has his public duties to think of; persons in the public service have not time to consider their own advantage," said the lady.

"Ah, how right Madame is! how fine is devotion to one's country!" cried the old man, with a grin which divided his long face into two halves, shrivelling up both. He laughed when his neighbour had passed, and went on laughing sardonically under his breath. Then his eyes fell upon Helen and the child. "Tiens! des Anglaises," he said.

Even Janey knew now that "des Anglaises" had something to do with her small self. She drew up her little person with conscious dignity, averting her head as she walked past.

"Bonjour, mes demoiselles," he said, and straightway addressed the alarmed Helen in a speech which drove all idea of amusement out of her head, comical though his grimaces were. To be addressed in so much French bewildered the girl, especially as he seemed to be asking something of her which she could not fathom. "Belle appartement, beau jardin, pension si on le veut."

What was it he was offering her? She blushed to the roots of her hair, and faltered in her English-French, "Pardonnez-moi, s'il vous plaît. Mon père n'est pas ici. Je ne sais pas. Mon père est——"

Helen's words failed her. She pointed with much embarrassment along the road which her father had gone.

"Ah! Monsieur est là-bas? in the woods? Bien, bien, bien! I will wait for Monsieur," said the old man.

The girls quickened their steps as they got away from him.

"What does he want, Helen?" Janey said in great alarm.

"Oh, I think he wants us to lodge there," said the elder sister, scarcely less uncomfortable.

The little girl looked up in her face with a dismayed and frightened countenance. "Are we doing to stay here—always?" little Janey said.

The question appalled them both, but the one knew as little as the other how to answer it. They went on softly in the sudden gloom which this idea spread round them. To drop suddenly from the skies from one

new place into another, might be amusing enough for a little while; but to remain—always, as Janey said! Helen's imagination was scarcely less young than her little sister's. To-day and always were the only alternatives. They held each other fast by the hand, and walked along the village street, feeling a sudden dreariness steal over the whole scene. It had relapsed into its usual quiet, though there were ranges of tables outside the Lion d'Or, and the rival *auberge* on the other side of the street, to accommodate the thirsty visitors when they should return from the woods. In the distance the young ladies· from the château were disappearing round the corner. The woman who had been washing her vegetables had disappeared, but another had come out to help her who was chopping the wood. And the old man still stood at his door, peering up and down the village. It was strange to go on disturbing the silence, interrupting the sunshine, in a place so quiet; their steps seemed to send echoes through all the tranquil place.

"Is it always so quiet?" Helen asked timidly when they reached the Lion d'Or. The mistress of the house stood at the door, shading her eyes with her hand, and looking out for the return of the expected purchasers. She was a buxom woman, in a white cap, with long, heavy earrings and bright eyes.

"Does Mademoiselle think it so quiet?" she said. "Wait till they begin to come back. *Ma foi*, it is a crowd, a tumult. In half an hour we shall not know where to turn to find a seat that is unoccupied. Ah! the Vente des bois is a great day. There is nothing like it out of Paris. But in Paris it lasts continually, that is the difference. Mademoiselle has been in Paris?"

"Only for a day."

"Aha, that is nothing at all. Paris cannot be seen in so little time. The English go too quickly, if you will pardon me for saying so. Paris! figure to yourself that I was there, Mademoiselle, effectively there, for all of a month. I know Paris at my fingers' ends."

"Are the young ladies very nice," said Helen, hesitating—(she did not know how to say nice, that accommodating word. "Les jeunes dames, sont-elles très-agréables"—which even to her English ear did not sound right—was what she said)—"at the Château?"

"*Comment?*— ah! you would say the demoiselles who passed just now. Yes, not amiss. We do not find fault with them," said Madame Dupré, with a slight shrug of the shoulders ; " but speaking of Paris, Mademoiselle. Ah! if I could but have sent my Baptiste there, what a happiness! He might have been clerk in one of the best *magasins* on the Boulevard. But boys are obstinate beyond all things, beyond the very mules. He prefers his village, and the woods, and the *chasse*. He gives me a great deal of inquietude, my boy. Should he draw a bad number it will be an evil day for the Lion d'Or. There is always that hanging over us. When a poor woman has several sons, instead of being a help to her it is but opening the gates to evil. She who has one only may keep him safe. And what does it matter, when they are helpless children, how many sons you have, Mademoiselle? Till the *tirage* is over I shall never know a day's ease. Sometimes I think it is better to have no children at all, as old M. Goudron says."

" Is that old M. Goudron?" said Helen, pointing to the old man who still stood at his door and watched, with his red and yellow handkerchief tied round his head.

" He is what we call a *richard*, Mademoiselle, the most rich person in the village. He has so much that he thinks it is a crime to be poor; he thinks it is your fault, not circumstances. His poor little grand-daughter lives with him in that big house, and he leads her a life! Fancy, Mademoiselle, the poor girl loves my Baptiste : they have always had a fancy for each other ; and if the old man would give her a *dot* as he promised, and Baptiste drew a good number——"

" What is a good number ?" said Helen in her ignorance. She did not know what it meant. That the young man's fate should depend on the very insignificant fact whether he drew five or fifty was incomprehensible to Helen.

Madame Dupré on her side was equally incapable of understanding how any one could be ignorant on the subject of the conscription. It did not require a very strong inducement to make her talk. And she launched forthwith into an eloquent denunciation of the evils of the system. " A low number is a good number," she said ; " but figure to yourself, Mademoiselle, what will happen to me if it comes otherwise. Either my Baptiste marched away to the life of the *caserne*—such a life, such a life, *mon Dieu !* and though he is a good son, he is idle, it do not deny it, he loves to wander : it would be his destruction ; or all that we have taken from us to buy a substitute. Often it is a thousand francs, no less. Think of that,

Mademoiselle, a thousand francs ! and I but a poor widow with four children. When I think of it in the night my sleep goes from me. Certainly M. Goudron has reason. Children are the chief pleasures in our existence, but it is true that they are at the same time our torment, they are our cross that we must bear."

She lifted up the corner of her apron to her eye, but seeing under its shadow the first person of the crowd coming into sight, she returned at once to her business.

" Quick, Jeanne," she said—" the soup ! they come." And sure enough, the one figure was soon followed by others. Madame Dupré lost not another moment. She took the long rolls out of the basket and put them by every plate. She set upon the table at equal distances the *vin du pays*, which was given with the meal. Her long earrings swung in her ears with the vehemence of her movements, her cap strings floated in the air. She sent little Auguste, the little waiter, in three directions at once, and, wonderful to relate, he went. Auguste was ubiquitous ; he could carry any number of plates, full or empty, and a laden tray on four fingers of his extended hand. His feet, in their low shoes, twinkled over the floor like lightning. He was never still for a moment. The two girls stood looking on at all these arrangements till Madame Dupré ran against them. " Pardon me, mes demoiselles," she said, " you will be better up-stairs. When Monsieur your father comes back he will like to find you in your own apartments. The Lion d'Or is very well regulated, but there are *mauvais sujets* that will take more wine than is good for them. When the bustle is over Auguste shall mount up-stairs with the young ladies' breakfast."

This speech, delivered without one pause for breath, was very puzzling to Helen, who had only understood approximately. But she understood enough to lead Janey, very reluctant, up-stairs. And here they watched the return of the buyers, which went on for the next two hours, one group and another coming in till the whole village was overflowing. The most important among them had maps of the property, to which they referred, perpetually pointing out to one another the different lots, and quarrelling about the position of their bits of timber. Mr. Goulburn returned as he had gone away, with young Baptiste and Antoine discoursing to him on either side. He had the air, radiant and satisfied, of a man who had done a good morning's work. He

listened to all they said to him with a smile, but he did not accept Antoine's offers of guidance in the matter of cutting up the wood he had bought, or getting the best price for it. "We will talk of that afterwards, my good friends," he said. He was willing to hear what they said to him, but he did not pledge himself to follow either. Meanwhile it was quite a gay scene from the windows of the Lion d'Or. The old man still stood at his door, exchanging a word here and there, and asking eager questions about the buyers. He had nothing to do with the old Count's wood, but to have something happening was a God-send to him. As for little Janey, the bustle in the street was delightful to her. She leaned out of the window, keeping Helen in terror. She called "Papa," making a pretty babyish grimace as she looked down upon him, watching her opportunity to drop something upon his head or his plate. However impatient of others, he had always toleration for Janey's freaks. Her countenance was as gay as that of the happiest child in Christendom; and his was bright with satisfaction and pleasure. It was not possible to Helen to change so easily. She gazed upon the happiness in both their faces with an envy that perhaps had a little disdain in it. How easily they threw over their burdens, while she—— And once more it became apparent to Helen that they were very likely to remain a long time at Latour.

CHAPTER VII.

"I HAVE bought a corner of the wood; I could not resist the temptation. So far as I can see, I must be able to make my own out of it. Well, perhaps it was foolish; but I must do something, and there is no likelihood of loss, at least."

Thus he explained himself somewhat lamely, with a consciousness that what he was saying must sound very strange to her. What did Helen know about his plans, or whether it was foolish or not, and why should he have explained it to her? It alarmed her as much as anything else in the strange and terrible imbroglio through which she could see no light.

"Papa, I—— You said you were poor——"

"Poor! And you think it is inconsistent with poverty that I should buy a few miserable bits of wood? You have made great progress lately, Helen, to permit yourself to sit in judgment on your father."

She looked at him piteously, with an appeal in her face. "I don't know about it, papa; how can I know, or how can I sit in judgment? Will you please not tell me anything? Because I don't understand, and then it looks as if I understood."

"It seems to me that you are no better than a fool, Helen." But when he had said this he went away, and relieved her from the pressure of the new burden to which she was so unaccustomed. The excuse, the apology conveyed in his explanations, gave her a sense of confused misery, incongruity, impossibility, which was almost the worst of all. Oh, why had he ever told her anything? Why had he raised her against her will into that position in which she was forced more or less to judge against her will? She sat, when he had gone, at the window of the little room up-stairs, which was the best room in the Lion d'Or. The white curtains, it need not be said, were fixed fast as if they were glued to the window. To draw them aside would have been more terrible to Madame Dupré than to break a moral law; the one might have been condoned by public opinion, but the other! Helen sat within the primly-fixed muslin which veiled all the world without, and sometimes shed a few tears quietly, while she made an attempt to mend Janey's frock. It was not a handicraft she understood, but at least she could fasten the two gaping sides of a rent together, and that was always some good.

But Janey was enchanted with the corner of the wood which her father had bought. He took them to see it in the afternoon, Antoine and Baptiste both following— Antoine as the possible wood-cutter for the removal of the trees, Baptiste as the host and natural care-taker of the strangers. With the latter, Janey had already made great friends in her fashion. The means of communication between them was limited, but that has little to do with real amity. When there had been something in the conversation which pleased Janey, she left her father's hand, and came up running and smiling to this new ally. "N'est-ce pas, Monsieur Baptiste?" Janey cried, and the young fellow replied with a broad grin, "Oui, Mademoiselle." Janey's little laugh rang through the trees after every interpellation of this kind. It was an admirable joke, which pleased everybody. As for Antoine, he did his best to attract a similar confidence, but without any success. He was not young and smiling like his rival. He was a tall and powerful man, with the head of a brigand, black-eyed and black-bearded, and his smile was uneasy and unreal; but Baptiste was brown and curly, his hair all hyacinthine, his boyish moustache curling over a perpetual smile. And the road into the woods was so cheerful and bright, that no wonder Janey was delighted. The oaks had begun to blaze in red and brown; the feathery larches drooped their delicate branches against an illuminated background of autumn tints; big green laurels and hollies made solid towers of green among the varied copse. A few magnificent foxgloves still remaining threw up their shafts of flowers, and there was not a bit of brushwood that had not some cluster of scarlet haws or trailing russet of a bramble to make it bright. The corner which Mr. Goulburn had bought was like a little pine-forest in itself—a regiment of tall and even firs. The sun was slanting in upon the red and golden columns upon which the dense yet varied roof of green was supported. Underneath, the brown carpet of fallen foliage, years upon years of growth, made slippery elastic cushions, which, with here and there a bank of emerald moss breaking through, were warm and soft. There were projections of twisted roots to make thrones of, and a tinkle of an unseen rivulet close by filled the air with music, when it could be heard for the sighing and murmuring over-head as the wind swept through the boughs. "Oh, let us never do away again! let us stay here for ever and ever!" cried little Janey; and then her little voice rang off into peals of laughter as she called out, "N'est-ce pas, Monsieur Baptiste?" "Oui, ma bonne petite demoiselle," said Baptiste, with his genial grin. He did not understand a word, but what did that matter? Mr. Goulburn was touched by his child's enthusiasm. "We shall not stay for ever and ever, but we may stay a good long time, my little Janey," he said; "it is a pretty place and quiet. Even Helen thinks so, who is never pleased."

The same night, when they were rising from the table in the little *salle à manger* where they had just dined, the old man whom Helen and her little sister had seen in the village street came in with his hat in his hand. He came up to their father with elaborate politeness. "Monsieur will pardon me," he said. "I know what is required by persons *comme il faut*, and though I have nothing to say against my good neighbour Madame Dupré, yet it cannot be denied that the arrangements of the house leave much

to be desired. Would Monsieur do me the favour to look at my apartment which is to let? I have already had the honour of mentioning it to Mademoiselle. My house is the best house in Latour. There is a garden which is laid out after the best models. If Monsieur will permit me to show it to him, he will make me happy."

Mr. Goulburn had been puzzled by the preamble about the wants of persons *comme il faut*. Everything that was unknown was a little alarming to him; but he recovered his placidity when the word *appartement* met his ear. "It is true," he said, "the arrangements of the Lion d'Or leave much to be desired, as this gentleman says. Shall we go and inspect his house as he proposes? It would not be a bad thing to do."

"Oh, no, no, no," cried little Janey, like a little fury. This time her father was not so much touched by her opinion. He told her she was a little goose, and finally he went out himself with old M. Goudron, desiring severely that the heroine of the afternoon should be put to bed. The day is over early in October, and when the two girls went up to their room, and lighted their solitary candle, it was a great deal less cheerful than in the ruddy woods, with the sunshine penetrating between the tall columns of the pines. The rush-bottomed chairs groaned at every movement upon the wooden floor. There was no fire, though the evening was cold, and the candle threw but a miserable light upon the two little wooden beds and the humble furniture, of which there was so little. "I want to do home," sobbed little Janey as she went weeping to bed. And Helen sat down again, and put the two gaping mouths of the rent together; or, rather, finished the joining of them which she had begun in the morning. She felt that it was not very well done. The daughter of a millionaire, with all kinds of servants at her call, how was she to know how to mend her little sister's frock? If that had been all! Helen felt herself able to learn; but how to arrange into something that was comprehensible this jarred and broken thread of life she did not know. By-and-by the nightly noise began below, which had ceased to disturb little Janey's sleep. Madame Dupré kept good wine, and Baptiste was a favourite in the village. The men came in, in their heavy boots, and talked in voices louder than the clod-hoppers of an English village. Often Helen sprang to her feet and ran to the door, thinking there was some deadly quarrel. It was only Jean or Pierre more eloquent than usual. Opposite, at the Cheval Blanc, there was the same tumult; but the village round about these two noisy places was as silent as a sleeping city. It was too cold for the women to stand about the doors and have their evening gossip. Helen went to her window and peeped out by the side of the blind when she had finished her mending. She could see M. Goudron's house opposite, and her father standing in the moonlight outside the door. A little superstitious thrill ran through her, she could not tell why; and just then Antoine came up, and stood and talked. They came back to the inn together, the big hulking figure of the villager, in his blue blouse, towering over Mr. Goulburn. Helen did not like the man, but her dislike of him did not seem enough to account for the sense of alarm with which she saw them cross the street together. She was relieved when her father came into the light under the window and entered the Lion d'Or.

Old Goudron was one of those born fortune-makers whose gift is as little capable of being crushed by circumstances as is the genius of a poet. He would have amassed wealth on a desert island. He had dealt in every kind of merchandise in his day, and it was believed that the manner of his traffic had not been always blameless. He had gone through all the possible industries of the village, he had dealt in ship stores at Marseilles, in wine-casks at Dijon, he had pounced on a hundred small gainful speculations which only a keen microscopic eye, always intent on profit, could see. He had neglected nothing, overlooked nothing, by which a penny could be made. Even now that he was old, and the *richard* of the village, supposed to possess unbounded wealth, his eyes were as keenly open as ever to all the possibilities of adding to his store. When he stood at his door with the handkerchief tied about his head nothing escaped him. If a child dropped a sou on the road it was supposed that old Goudron picked it up. Money stuck to his fingers, the people said; they were half afraid of him, yet almost reverential of his genius. M. Goudron, however, with this one faculty, which is cosmopolitan, added others which belong more exclusively to his country. He scoffed at religion in all its forms, and he was republican of the republicans. He scoffed at most things, it is well to add. His long countenance, cut in two by the mockery of his characteristic grin, was that of a vulgar and mean Voltaire, always on the watch for an opportunity of reviling. Naturally such re-

mains of his family as were left to him did everything that in them lay to thwart all the objects of his life. His children were dead, and he had but three grandchildren remaining to him in the world. Of these, two girls lived with him in his house, suffered all his caprices, and crossed him in every instinct of his nature; and the remaining one, his son's son, his natural representative, was a spendthrift and good-for-nothing, abroad somewhere in the world, of whom the old man knew nothing, except that he was sure to turn up some time to reclaim his part of the succession, from which, according to French law, he could not be shut out. Thus M. Goudron knew that his cherished money, when he left it behind him, would go to Blanchette, the girl who wanted to marry Baptiste Dupré without a sou; and to Ursule, who had a *vocation*, and was bent on becoming a nun; and to Léon, who was a good-for-nothing, and spent every penny he could get before he earned it. This was not a pleasant prospect for the old *richard*. Perhaps it embittered him against the world. It certainly made life so much the harder for the two poor girls who were his descendants, but who had no sympathy with him. Though he was so rich, they were exactly like the other cottage girls of Latour. Margot, the good woman who lived in the next cottage, came in, before she attended to her own household, to do what was wanted for M. Goudron's lodgers, but Blanchette and Ursule, though they were heiresses, did all the household work in their own apartment up-stairs. Margot's children chopped the wood and drew the water, but it was Ursule who kept the house in that chill and waxy cleanliness which is the French ideal, and Blanchette who cooked and washed and served the table. Work, indeed, is reduced to its easiest proportions in a house where there are only as many rooms as are absolutely wanted, and no carpets in these rooms; and where the kitchen fire is a little pan of charcoal, capable of being lighted or extinguished in a moment. Margot, with her smiling brown face and her white cap, did all this for the lodgers down-stairs. She swept their bare salon at an unusually early hour in the morning, waking the girls by the vigorous sounds of her broom, and dusted the long formal candelabra and large bronze clock which half covered the old mirror over the chimney-piece. When they came in on the first morning there was a log blazing in the wide chimney, sending its ruddy sparks and almost all the warmth it produced up

that vast aperture. Janey coming in, flew to the fire with delight, putting her little hands out to the ruddy glow. " It is as nice as the forest," Janey said ; " I am so glad we came here !" Margot let her brush of feathers drop, and folded her arms, and looked on with a broad smile.

"The little one is charming," she said. "She is not so tranquil, Mademoiselle, saving your respect, as most of you other English. Do you never talk, what we call *causer*, among yourselves?"

" I do not know what is the difference between *parler* and *causer*," said Helen.

" Ah, Mademoiselle, such a difference ! I am too ignorant to explain ; one feels it, one does not know how to describe. *Tenez !* if Mademoiselle knew the young persons upstairs—Ursule, who is as good as a little saint, she has her mind full of religion, she is always serious. Mademoiselle knows that she has a *vocation*, and but for that old Père Goudron, who is Voltairian, who is—hush ! he has ears that go over all the house. Bien ! Ursule talks, *elle parle;* but her sister, little Blanchette, who is the little merry one, she

who is always singing, she who chatters, chatters all day long, and never is quiet—*elle cause.* Now Mademoiselle will see the difference. And perhaps the English, too, *causent,* though we never hear them, when they are at home, as we are here."

" It is because we only know a few words," said Helen. " I should like to *causer* like Mademoiselle Blanchette, but——"

" Ah !" cried Margot, " here is a beginning ! Mademoiselle is ten times more pretty when her face lights up. When we allow ourselves to criticize, this is what we say of the English—' They are too serious; they have what we call *figures de bois*.' When one chatters, when one smiles, all is changed. She is charming, *la petite.*"

" What is she saying about *la petite?*" said Janey. " *La petite*, that is me ! I want to know what she says."

" Je dis que vous êtes charmante, Mademoiselle," cried Margot, with a laugh. " You see I understand the English. If the little demoiselle will condescend to amuse herself with my little Marion and Petit-Jean, she will soon learn to chatter like the rest. Monsieur your father speaks very good French, and I hear that he knows himself in affairs to perfection, Mademoiselle. They say he had the best bargain of all in the Vente des bois, and that he will make enormously by it. Ah, the English, they are the people for affairs!" said Margot admiringly. "But to imagine that one like Monsieur should have taken the trouble to come all this way to little Latour for the Vente des bois! That shows how the English always have their wits about them, while we, who are on the spot, and who ought to know, we are so *bête* we let those good bargains slip out of our hands."

"We did not hear of it in England," said Helen; "we were travelling——"

"Ah! and one knows how to join affairs to one's pleasure when one is English. It is extraordinary; they never forget themselves," Margot said. "But Monsieur is rich?" she added interrogatively. "It makes nothing to him to gain a little, to take the profits out of another's hands. It is *pour s'amuser*, to distract himself, to forget the ennui which is peculiar to the English."

"We were once rich," said Helen, "but we are not rich now; Papa says so. And we have no ennui, as you call it, in England," she cried indignantly.

Margot smiled; she could forgive the patriotic denial, but she was aware that she knew better. "All the same," she said, "it must be sad to live in a perpetual fog and never to see the sun. For that I could never support your England, notwithstanding all that you have there. Of what use is wealth when you cannot see the sky?" said Margot. Helen was too indignant to reply.

But in the course of the first day she got a great deal of information from Margot, who told her all about the young ladies at the Château, who talked English "comme deux diablesses," the woman said—and who were indeed English-mad, and betrothed, one of them, to an Englishman. When Helen asked once more in her halting French whether they were "très-agréables," meaning "very nice," Margot answered with a shrug of her shoulders—

"I do not know anything to the contrary. What does that matter to us others if the aristocrats are *agréable* or not? They are not as we are, they are not of us. They have got their château and their *bois*, and all that, though many people think they have no right, and should not be allowed to retain it. But I say to my man, What is that to us? We have not the money to buy it. Let them stay. Madame la Comtesse is better than

old Père Goudron, who would buy it all if it were taken away from them. So why should we interfere? that is what I always say——"

"Interfere!" said Helen, not knowing what to think.

"Jacques, who is my man, is not always of my opinion, Mademoiselle. He says, why should there be a château for one and a little cabin for another? But I say, 'Hold thy tongue, *mon homme*. How would it advantage thee?' It is hard, nevertheless," said Margot, "that we should have to go and buy our own woods to warm us in the winter. The trees were not made by M. le Comte; they are there for all the world. Yet we must spend our little money, and go to the Vente, and pay for what has grown out of the earth! This is an injustice. When anything passes through a *fabrique* and is manufactured, I allow that it should be paid for; but that which grows by itself, which comes out of the ground, that is different. Figure to yourself that I am talking politics to the English young lady. *Va*, Margot, thou art a fool for thy pains! Naturally Mademoiselle is Conservative—she loves the aristocrats, like all her nation?"

"I don't know," said Helen, surprised. She had heard her father rail against aristocrats, but she had understood that it was because the great people round Fareham had been uncivil. She had never supposed the existence of such a feeling in a cottage, and it puzzled her too much to make any reply possible. "But surely——" she began, then stopped, for she was not very sure of anything in French, and even in English could not venture upon a political argument. She returned with some difficulty and discomfort to the original question.

"The young ladies at the Château, are they not good to the poor?"

"Oh, *les pauvres!* Yes, yes; they are kind enough. When one is ill they will come and demand, 'What can one do for you?' It is true, Mademoiselle; but one does not like to have it thus forced upon one brutally that others are better off than one's self. That humbles you. I prefer, for my part, that they should not interfere. *Assez!* let us talk of something else," said Margot, taking up her *plumet*, which in her fervour she had allowed to drop from her hand. This was the worst of Margot's ministrations. When she became interested in the conversation, the feather-brush always dropped and the dusting was suspended. As for Helen, she felt her world widening around her. She forgot the strange sentiments she had been hearing, and the strange position in which she found herself. On one hand there was little Blanchette with her story, and on the other the young ladies at the château who spoke English. Her heart filled with excitement and hope. They were nothing to her, but they opened once more the ordinary world, and delivered her from her own tribulations and thoughts.

CHAPTER VIII.

HELEN and her little sister were left very much to themselves for some time after they settled in M. Goudron's house, and the village life going on round them soon became interesting and important to the strangers. Little Janey played all day long with Marie

and Petit-Jean, and acquired a Burgundian accent, and an ease of speech much beyond that of Helen, who still talked as with a shadow behind her of her governess, and was tremulous about her genders, and afraid of the subjunctive mood. It was wonderful how soon they came to know the stories which hid under each little thatched roof. Though Helen did not dare in the face of public opinion to unfasten the closely strained curtain that covered her windows, she managed to draw its fulness towards the centre, leaving a little corner by which she could see what was going on. The chief thing she saw, it must be allowed, was old Goudron standing at the door watching everything that went on

with his hungry old eyes, and grinning with malicious pleasure at every mishap. Nothing escaped the old man, and his grin was the chief thing in Latour which soured the milk of human kindness, made the good wives cross, they could not tell why, and exasperated the men. He was always there with malignant and mocking words whatever happened, to say that " I told you so "—which makes every misfortune a little more unbearable ;—" if you had listened to me." The house next door was the only house in the village which made any pretentions to gentility. M. le Précepteur who lived in it was not a schoolmaster, as the English reader may suppose, but the collector of taxes, a government employé,

who held on with a very stern clutch to the skirts of the aristocracy as a man well born, with a wife who found herself sadly out of place in this desert. When Madame went by in her pretty toilettes, M. Goudron had always a jibe. The public virtue of M. le Précepteur, and his devotion to the country, was his favourite subject. " Quoi, Madame ! it is too much to have an old Roman for a husband. Again you go out alone," he would say. Madame knew that her irreproachable husband was playing billiards at the moment, thinking very little of public duty and still less of the enormity of leaving her to go out alone, but she held up her head and smiled disdainfully. " In our class,

Monsieur," she said, "we are trained from
our cradles to recognise that each has
their share of duty—society for the women,
but for the men the country. It is difficult, I am aware, to make it comprehensible among the bourgeois," she added,
sweeping past with the sweetest smile. Old
Goudron grinned, but he had his match.
Helen watched their passages of arms daily.
The employé's wife was a good mother and
an excellent housewife, but neither for home
nor children would she have relinquished the
grandeur of her caste. She paid visits at the
Château ; she patronised the Curé ; and
visited the good sisters who kept their little
school at the other end of the village ; and
maintained her little social circle with the
stateliness of a duchess. Once a week she
had her little reception, which was attended by
M. le Curé, M. le Vicaire (for it was a large
parish), and the notary. Once a week she
and her husband dined at the Château.
Regularly as the weeks came round were
these social rules observed, for, as she justly
remarked, "Without society one vegetates,
one does not live." It was much in the
mind of this one representative of high life in
Latour to open her doors to the strangers.
The father's appearance was perfectly comme
il faut, and though Helen was shy she had
still the air of a young person who had been
instructed, and might have been née, like
Madame herself.

Nobody else in Latour had a salon or the
ghost of a salon. But Helen, peeping from
her corner, soon got to know which of the
cottage wives looked out anxiously for the
return of their husbands, and which reposed
with pride and calm upon the certainty of
Jean or Jacques' sobriety and good behaviour.
She began to know the different clank of the
sabots, from the little patter of the children,
in their dark blue homespun frocks and close
little caps, to the heavy resounding tread of
the big boys and men. She knew M. le
Curé's measured step, and the pause he
made to leave his wooden overshoes behind
when he went in to see a sick man ; and the
brisker little trot of M. le Vicaire, who had
been in the war, and who was a fiery little
martyr, tramping leagues off to the edge of
the parish to see the sick or any one who
called for his aid. On Monday every week
M. le Curé went to the Château to say a
mass for the old Count in the little chapel,
and stayed afterwards to take his déjeuner,
the second breakfast, which till all these
masses were over was the first meal for the
good Curé. It was on Thursday that the

priest and the Précepteur and his wife dined
at the Château of Latour, and on Sunday
was the reception of Madame next door. On
Sunday all the village was astir. There was
a great deal going on in the church in the
morning, and a tolerable amount of people
there, a far larger number than was justified
by the professions of the villagers, who dis-
owned all the habits of piety and made themselves out much less Christian than they were.
It is the fashion to be religious in the upper
classes, and all who would aspire to belong
to them in France ; and it is the fashion
among the peasantry to fear the Church ;
yet notwithstanding, there were a great many
people at the high mass, wherever they came
from. M. le Précepteur was there with his
wife in her prettiest toilette, and their little
girl as fine as a little girl could be; and M. le
Maire and the adjoint both thought it expedient to set a good example to the community. But it was only the morning that
the best of Catholics thought it necessary to
devote to the services of religion. Even
Madame la Comtesse at the Château, though
orthodox to the fingers' tips, took care to
assure her guests that vespers were not a
duty, pas obligatoire, and in the afternoon and
evening all the merriment of the village, such
as it was, was in full swing. The Lion d'Or
and the Cheval Blanc were both full, and in a
large loft belonging to the former there was
dancing, which Helen and Janey watched
with a fearful joy through the open window.
To be able to see this even at a distance was
an amusement they had not hoped for : yet
Helen was very uneasy as to whether it was
justifiable on Sunday even to look on at a
dance. But it was not very riotous dancing,
or even very gay, as we are led to suppose
the amusements of our gayer neighbours
are. They took their pleasure very seriously,
these Burgundian peasants, just as our own
country folks do. The violinist of the village
had no great variety of music in his repertoire,
and the peasant couples, solemnly circling
round and round with their hands on each
others' shoulders, displayed little of that
characteristic gaiety of France which we
hear so much about. Down below, in front
of the windows on the benches outside,
the men drank steadily and talked, till it
became too cold, while the women sitting
by, knitting their stockings, sometimes threw
in a word. They made a great deal more
noise than similar assemblies do in England, but there was not much more mirth.
Very often a passing show, a travelling
establishment of pedlar's wares—a " Cheap

Jack," or at the worst a dentist in a triumphal car, making their last rounds before the winter set in, would arrive at Latour, and this made Sunday very piquant, before everything succumbed under the chills of the declining season. Madame Dupré at the Lion d'Or, in her whitest cap, with her long earrings, occupied the large chair on these Sundays, leaving the waiting to Auguste, and Baptiste, and Jeanne from the kitchen, whose holiday it was to emerge from that hot and stifling place, putting also long earrings in her ears, and a cap that might have been starched in Paris, it was so *comme il faut*. Jeanne liked to show herself in the *salle* among all the people on these Sunday nights. But Baptiste for his part was always seeking to get away. He stole up to the dancing-room to have one waltz with his Blanchette, then rushed down to get a *chope* for Jean Pierre, or a new bottle of *piquette* for Père Roussel, or the absinthe which the little city clerk, who had come to help M. le Notaire, thought it fine to call for. And thus the Sunday evenings went on. Madame la Comtesse would have liked to shut up the *auberges* and have Sunday kept as in England, if she could ; and Madame Vincent, the Précepteur's wife, had fixed her reception for Sunday in order to prevent her husband and the notary from patronising the vulgar popular meeting in the Lion d'Or. But neither of these great ladies influenced the village. The first it regarded as a hostile power, whom to thwart was one of the first of its duties, the other as a laughing-stock.

Mr. Goulburn walked about the village for the first Sunday evening, and amused himself, while his daughters at the window saw all the rude little frolicking at a distance— the dancing-room with its open windows, the oil lamps burning hot and smoky in the gloom, the dancers gyrating, not always in time, to the squeak of the village fiddle ; and down below, the light in the windows of the *salle* at the Lion d'Or broken by the figures of the people who sat outside. The girls were not so soon bored as he was. He was a man who liked to be popular, as has been said. He went in to pay his respects to Madame Dupré and made her his little compliments.

"All the world is here," he said, "to-night. I find you on your throne, Madame, the queen of the village."

Madame Dupré was so pleased that she accorded him a civility shown to few. She got up to offer him a seat and called to Baptiste to bring her a certain precious little bottle.

"Monsieur must taste it—it is genuine,"

she said ; "it was brought me from the hands of the monks who have the secret."

"Ah, the monks," some one said, "they like to keep all the good things to themselves."

"And with good reason," said Mr. Goulburn. "Could I make anything so good as this, certainly I should keep it to myself."

This *mot* had a little *succès* in the company which pleased its author. It is hard to say how far down we will go for applause without any sense of lowering ourselves. Praise is always pleasant.

"Monsieur has reason," said Madame Dupré. "I am not *dévote*, but now and then I like to hear one who will say a good word for the clergy."

Old M. Goudron, who was sitting by, took his cigar out of his mouth.

"Madame is too good," said the old man ; "she would say a good word for the devil, if there is such a person, and if he were a customer at the Lion d'Or."

"The clergy are no customers of mine, nor do I hold with them any more than you do," Madame Dupré began, with rising colour, when the Englishman poured oil on the waves.

"In my country," he said, "the clergy are not a separate class as in yours. They marry and live like other men ; but no one in England speaks of them as you do here in France. They do a great deal of good among us. They take care of the poor."

"Pah ! a married priest !" cried Madame Dupré, with an expression of disgust. "I am no bigot, but I could not put up with that."

"And as for what Monsieur says about the poor," cried M. Goudron, "there ought not to be any poor. A man who wants help, who cannot keep himself alive, there is no place for him in this world."

At this a little murmur rose, and one of the silent spectators spoke. "We are all poor," he said, "and when there is a bad harvest, or a bad winter, or illness in the house, how are we to live without the help of a kind hand?"

"Ah, it is you, Paul le Roux ; every one knows why you speak. There is solidarity between the enemies of mankind, the priest and the aristocrat ; they have but one end. It is for this they wander about the village to take persons at a disadvantage who may happen to be badly off. You do not see how their charity is an impudence. What, give you their crumbs, and their fragments! 'Take what falls from my table, I am better than thou.' It is an insult—such an insult," old Goudron said suddenly, with the grin that divided his face in two, "as I never would venture to offer to any neighbours of mine."

At this there was a general laugh. "Père Goudron," said some one from the window, "will never fail in respect to his neighbours in that way."

"Never!" cried the old man with his malignant grin.

In the meantime young Baptiste had escaped from the table and the drinking, and had gone back to the dancers, who were now beginning to disperse. He went across the street with his Blanchette and her friends, and secure in the occupation of both their parents, talked for half a happy hour with her at the door. When he bade her good night at last, and little Blanchette went in with the blush on her cheeks, Helen, somewhat pale from her vigil, was standing at the door of the sitting-room. "Will you come in?" she said. She had been sitting there a long time alone, since Janey went to bed, watching the dancers, and listening to the squeak of the fiddle and the hum of all the voices. It was not a kind of merry-making which Helen could have shared; yet to see people enjoying themselves, and to sit alone and look from a distance at their pleasure, is sad when one is young. She was glad to see the bright countenance of the other girl, who was in the midst of all that little agitation of youthful life from which she was herself shut out. There was but one candle in the bare little salon, and that was put away in a corner not to interrupt the sight of the village gaiety outside. Blanchette came in, proud of the invitation, and looked out with great sympathy upon the scene she had herself left, where now the dancing figures were fewer and more irregular, and the lights more smoky and lurid than ever.

"Was Mademoiselle looking at us all the time?" she said; and then she suddenly took and kissed with fervour, to Helen's great surprise, her unwilling hand. "Mon dieu!" said little Blanchette, "but how sad for Mademoiselle!"

"Oh, thanks," cried Helen, much confused and not knowing what to do. She would have liked to kiss the little girl who felt for her, but she was too shy to do this. "It amused me very much," she said with a little sigh—perhaps she had scarcely thought that her amusement was sad till Blanchette suggested it. "I think I saw you dancing with Baptiste."

"Oh, yes, Mademoiselle. He came as often as he could. Mademoiselle knows that we are fiancés."

"Yes; but you are too young to be married," Helen said.

"Does Mademoiselle think so? Baptiste is almost twenty. Provided that he draws a good number, that is all we have to hope for. Will Mademoiselle say a little prayer for us when the moment comes? Ursule has promised a candle to St. Hubert if all goes well. Ursule has no wishes for herself. She is a saint upon earth. All that she asks from heaven is for me."

"But she is only a very little older than you are. Why should she have no wishes for herself?"

"Mademoiselle, she has a vocation," said Blanchette with awe; the candle shone back, doubled and reflected in those twin mirrors, from her eyes. The gravity on her face brought out all its sweetness—a little face all alive with love and hope and reverential admiration and faith. Helen felt her own passiveness all the more from the contrast. She felt half ashamed of her ignorance, and of standing, as she did, outside of all this world so full of life.

"What is a vocation?" she said.

"Does not Mademoiselle know? A vocation is something one does not talk of carelessly, as we are talking; it is too sacred, when it is a true vocation. She would have been at the Sacré Cœur now, had not grandpapa been so—— Figure to yourself, Mademoiselle, that grandpapa is very violent against the Church. He hates even the good sisters who are so kind. When M. le Curé passes he spits on the ground. It is terrible," cried Blanchette with tears in her eyes, "to be so old and to be like that. If Baptiste draws a good number, he will not be able to refuse that we should marry," she added very seriously, too grave for blushing, "and then perhaps my poor Ursule—— The holy mother will take her without dot, they have such faith in her; but she would not leave me alone with the grandfather. Provided only that Baptiste draws a good number!" the girl said, clasping her hands.

"Surely, surely he will!" Helen said fervently.

Little Blanchette shook her head. "If things would happen because we wish them to happen!" she said—and then she added, "Baptiste, perhaps, has been a little idle, Mademoiselle; but all Latour wishes him well, and the ladies of the Sacré Cœur have promised to make a neuvaine for us. They would do anything for Ursule's sister. I wish I had a little more faith, Mademoiselle," she said, shaking her head once more.

Helen had that vague confidence that what is desired must happen, which is common to the very young, when their own feelings are not so deeply concerned as to make them despondent; and though she could not possibly know anything about it, and her assurances that all would be well were absolutely worthless, still they consoled Blanchette, who was very grateful for the interest shown in her, and cried, and smiled, and declared Mademoiselle to be an angel. This was not unpleasant on the other hand to the lonely little Englishwoman. To be sure Blanchette was not a lady, but she was a girl, and the freemasonry of youth is warm. Helen got quite excited as she speculated upon the chances which involved the happiness of this young pair. She herself knew nothing of such agitations. She felt to herself like a very pale little shadow standing by looking on, while the others were involved in all those hopes and fears. She too had been plunged into a stormy sea, but it was very different from this one; Helen did not understand the change in her own life, and notwithstanding all that her father had said could not feel at all sure that this mysterious chapter might not end as it began, and Fareham and its splendours reappear again in her existence. But as she sat down in the semi-darkness after Blanchette had left her, her mind followed an altogether different line of thinking. Blanchette was the perennial heroine of human story. All the romances, all the poetry were occupied with troubles like hers. None of them took any interest in the fate of a girl whose father was the cause of her misfortunes, and with whose griefs no warmer thought of possible happiness was twisted. She was altogether in the shadow, and sympathy was not for her. She had not even a chance of sympathy without a complaint, without, perhaps, betraying her father, which was impossible. But with Blanchette everybody sympathised, even the ladies of the Sacré Cœur who might be expected to be not too favourable to marriage. Helen knew nothing of this phase of life. She wondered, with a shy alarm at her own thoughts, if, as the novels said, something of the kind happened in everybody's experience? The thought made her laugh faintly by herself, and made her blush, though without the slightest reason; and then suddenly there came before her, like a scene in a theatre, the table-d'hôte at Sainte-Barbe, and the young stranger who startled her by his recognition, and who had been so glad to see her. Why had he been so glad to see her? A little

tremble ran over Helen, a flush to her face, and she laughed again, this time more faintly than ever, then sprang up and took down the candle from the old-fashioned marble-topped sideboard in the corner, and put it on the table, and got her book. She had been reading a pious French book which she had found in her room, because it was Sunday; it was not very engrossing. Her thoughts strayed away from it in spite of herself. But she tried her best to hold them fast and read very steadily. By-and-by the sounds outside lessened and withdrew, and steps could be heard passing, one group after another taking their way home. The day of leisure was over, and to-morrow the work would begin once more. Helen had begun to watch for her father's step among the heavier ones outside, when Blanchette suddenly put her head within the door.

"Mademoiselle," she cried, breathless, "here is Monsieur coming home, and Antoine Roussel. Baptiste told me that I ought to warn you. One does not like to say ill of one's neighbours, but Antoine is a *mauvais sujet*. All the village says so. One cannot trust him. If Mademoiselle were to say as much to Monsieur son père?—and good night—good night—and a thousand times thanks, ma bonne et chère demoiselle."

Her head disappeared as quickly as it had come. Helen was a little confused by the sudden warning, by the complications of the language with which she was still so unfamiliar. To be addressed in the third person still mystified her a little, and so did *Monsieur son père*. But she had a strong youthful prejudice against Antoine, who followed her father about everywhere, and whom Janey could not bear. "But what, will papa care?" she said to herself, though indeed it was possible that he might care for the altogether causeless prejudice of little Janey, if not for any remonstrance of hers.

CHAPTER IX.

IT is curious with what ease we adapt ourselves to the completest change in the very foundations of life; a little difference is vexatious and irritating while a revolution which carries us away from our own identity, substituting a new routine, an entirely altered existence, is comparatively easy. Mr. Goulburn, whose affairs had been of the vastest, who had been in the full turmoil of life, in the midst of society and excitement, held at the highest strain, and running the most tremendous risks, fell into the life of the village with an ease which bewildered himself.

He could not comprehend the soothing influences of the calm and good order, the silence and dulness which all at once enveloped him like a cloud. Even Montdard was farther off from Latour than any part of the civilised world is from London. Amid the woods of the Haute Bourgogne it was more difficult to realise what went on ten leagues off, than it was in England to understand how all the great affairs of the world were going. He had bought that clump of pine-trees in a momentary sympathy with the excitement of the country, and with a notion brought from the old life which he had abandoned, that it was a good thing to have something to occupy him. But he was not so keen even about his fir-trees as he had expected to be. The leisurely habits of the country got possession of him. He walked to the woods and looked at them, then came home to breakfast, then amused himself with calculating the profit to be made of them, and all that could be done. Never before in his active life had he been out of the world. He was so now, and the distance confused all his faculties. He had lost sight of everything he knew, of all that he had calculated upon, of all the influences which had affected him before. The people about, in the *cabarets*, by the roadside, talked politics indeed, but their discussions seemed so fantastic and unreal to the constitutional Englishman, that they rather increased than lessened his sense that he was out of the world altogether, drifted into some other life. Those wild theories of universal right, broken lights of communism, all the more lurid because of the passion of proprietorship with which they were mixed ; the hatred of the aristocrats ; the fear of the Church ; all those prejudices which were so extraordinary to his mind, looked to him like something got up for his admiration and bewilderment, scenes at the theatre, which not even the players themselves could believe in. They amused him greatly, being all sham as he thought, dramatic exhibitions natural to the French character ; he for one was not taken in by them ; but they convinced him more of the unreality of this life. He had got into some enchanter's cave, some lotus island ; he did not know at all what was going on outside. Was he a man for whom there was search being made, and with a price upon his head ? or had he dropped out of all agitations whatsoever, out of knowledge of the world ? He could not tell ; he had not seen a *Times* since he had left London. One terrible fit of alarm he had gone through at Sainte-Barbe. But Charley Ashton certainly could not have

known anything, or he would have let it somehow appear in his looks, even if he had taken no ulterior steps. And how could any one, however great an offender, however well known to the world, be found in this place, which was not in the world ? The idea seemed absurd. Then Mr. Goulburn amused himself with his calculations about the wood. He was not in any danger from Antoine. A peasant and poacher of the rudest French type was not very likely to take in a man of the world ; and he had no more intention of leaving the wood-cutting in Antoine's hands than of doing it himself.

As for little Janey, she was as happy as the day was long, with little Marie from the cottage next door, and Petit-Jean. Her French bubbled up like a little fountain, all mingled with laughter. It was so funny to talk like the little French children, Janey thought ; and no doubt they too could talk English like her if they would take the trouble. Helen, too, settled down as if she had been to the manner born. She, who had scarcely ever threaded a needle for herself, mended the rents in Janey's frocks, and took pleasure in it. She learned from Blanchette how to knit, and began to make warm stockings for her little sister. She taught Janey her letters every morning. She had a great deal to do, to supplement Margot's exertions with the feather-brush, and arrange everything as well as she could, the meals and all the details of the house. And by-and-by Helen began to forget the strange way in which this change had been accomplished. She forgot that midnight flight, the dismal journey, the fugitive's career from place to place. She could scarcely have told any one what it was that had brought them to Latour. Had they meant to come to Latour when they left England ? Helen could not tell. She was embarrassed, bewildered by the question, though it was she who put it to herself. She had lived a life so retired and quiet in England, that she had nobody to regret except Miss Temple, who had married Mr. Ashton ; but this marriage had happened nearly a year ago, and Helen had spent all the summer alone. The time we spend alone goes so slowly. She had lived like a young hermit in the great house ; even Janey she had only seen when Nurse thought proper. She had nothing to do, nothing to live by, nobody to think of. She had been awoke all at once from that feeble dream of existence by the thunder-clap of the sudden flight. And now she found herself like one who has fallen from a great height, or recovered from a severe illness, or been picked up out of the sea—living and thankful to be living, accustoming herself to this surprising reality of existence, so true after so much that was not true. Helen's intellect had not very many requirements, and such as it had could be supplied by that perennial fountain of dreams which makes up for so much that is lacking in youth. She had no books to read, but she told herself a long and endless fable through all the silent hours, so much the more enthralling that she was always in it, the doer, or the cause of the doing, present in all its succeeding scenes.

The ruddy October weather had come to an end, and November had begun to close in, dark and heavy, when the next incident occurred in Helen's life. This was when she made the acquaintance of the young ladies at the Château, who had looked very wistfully at her for a long time when they met her, before they finally broke the ice. Helen herself had thought it was " her place " to await overtures, not to make any attempt at a beginning, which ought to come from the other side. It was the morning after the first snow, when everything was white around Latour, the trees hanging heavy with a load of crystals, the path sparkling underneath their feet. Very few, indeed, were the people who were out to brave it. Most of the villagers had got in their stock of wood, and collected their potatoes, their winter supply of vegetables ; no improvident buying from day to day, except by the poorest and least respectable of the population, was known at Latour. Those who had gardens, or little farms, had stored up all their treasures for the severe season. A great number of the men were busy in the woods, the women kept indoors. Till evening, when the men came home, there was scarcely a soul visible in the village; then there was a little stir, a sound of heavy feet, and all was quiet again. Blanchette shivered when she saw that Helen had prepared to go out—" Mademoiselle will die of the cold," she said; " and *la petite!* it is to kill her."

"But Ursule has been at mass as usual," said Helen, with a little triumph, seeing the prints of a little pair of sabots in the snow. " That is a different thing, that is *obligatoire,*" Blanchette said, with great gravity. "Mademoiselle knows that my sister is almost a religious ; and when it is so, what does it matter ? cold or wet, is there not the *bon Dieu* to take care of you ? "

" The *bon Dieu* takes care of us all," said Helen.

She was a Protestant, which, though no one knew what it was, was certainly not a Christian, and, therefore, had no particular right to be cared for by God. Still Blanchette did not object to this supernatural shield for Helen. She only shook her head as they left the door. These uncovenanted mercies, though always to be hoped for, are risky; whereas in the case of Ursule, there could be no doubt, on all sides, of the perfect security of the guarantees. Janey was delighted to feel the crisp and dazzling snow under her little feet ; she ran and danced upon it, stamping on the hard shining surface. " It is like a big, big cake," said Janey, " and me the little lady on it. Don't you know, Helen, the little lady with the stick ? "

It was a Twelfth-Day cake of which Janey was thinking, and Helen could not help recollecting the very cake which had kept a tender place in her little sister's thoughts. It was one which had figured at the school treat organized by Miss Temple, before she went away and married.

" Do you remember the little lady, Janey?"

" She turned round and round," said the child; "she had a stick and pointed. Let me get a stick and point too."

What a different scene came before Helen's eyes! the schoolroom at Fareham all decked with holly, the great white cake sparkling like the snow, the eager children drawing their characters ; and in the midst of the party a splendid shy little person wrapped in furs, who was the giver of the feast, and to whom everybody looked with so much desire that she should be pleased. She thought she could hear the horses pawing with impatience at the door, and see little Janey flushed with excitement, wrapped in the softest satin-quilted mantle, carried out by the biggest of footmen to the most luxurious of carriages. Helen laughed softly to herself—was it a dream ? She thought of it as Cinderella might have thought of her ball had there been no young prince in it, nothing to make the episode of special importance. Was it really true ? And it was at this moment, while Janey was pirouetting round and round with the wand in her hand, and when Helen had just laughed to herself at the strange recollection of the past, which was so unlike the present—that the two Demoiselles de Vieux-bois came suddenly round the corner and met them. There was a little pause on both sides. An " Oh ! " of startled expectation came to Helen's Britannic lips, and the two young Frenchwomen swerved for a moment, then stopped and held a hurried consultation. Then one of them ad-

vanced with pretty hesitation, a blush and a smile.

"Pardon, Mademoiselle," she said; then added in very passable English, "we have wished to call, but our mamma has been sick, and we were doubtful to come alone. Perhaps you will let us make friends now?"

"Oh, I shall be so glad," cried Helen, putting out her hands shyly, with a sudden flash of light and colour coming to her face. They had thought the English miss, like all English misses, pale and cold.

"I told you so," said the one to the other. "I am Cécile de Vieux-bois, and my sister is Thérèse. We have wanted so much to speak to you. You are English, and we have such dear friends in England."

"She has her *fiancé* there," said the other, laughing. "She is going to be English herself."

"Et peut-être toi aussi," said Cécile, half reproachfully, in an under-tone.

"*Crois pas,*" said the youngest, shaking her head. She caught Janey up and gave her a sudden kiss. "This little one is delicious," she said, translating her native idiom into English. "We have so much remarked her in church, everywhere; and you too, Miss——" she added anxiously, lest Helen's feelings should be hurt. "How shall we call you? Miss——"

Helen's face grew scarlet. She had never been brought face to face before with this terrible difficulty. Her name had been of no importance in Latour. If her father called himself by one name or another she knew nothing of it. Mademoiselle was enough for everything.

"Please do not say miss at all," she said, the tears (and how sharp they were, like fire more than water!) coming to her eyes. "I am Helen, and she is little Janey. Will you call us so?"

"But it will not be *comme il faut* to call you Helen the first time we see you, without either miss or mademoiselle."

"We don't say miss in England," said Helen stoutly; "no one says it who is *comme il faut*, only the servants."

The two French girls looked at each other with a little surprise—perhaps they did not like to be supposed ignorant on this point; or perhaps the fervour of Helen's protest struck them, though they could not tell what it meant. But they were too well-bred to make any further difficulty. "Do you like our poor little Latour?" said Cécile. "It is so strange to us to see any new faces here. We shall be so happy to have you all the long winter—that is, if you are going to stay."

It was Cécile who spoke the best English. The younger one was playing with Janey, and chattering in a mixture of languages which amused and suited them both. Cécile and Helen walked on demurely side by side. "We shall stay if—if papa likes it," she said.

"Monsieur your father is not strong?" said Cécile, with a sympathetic look. "I said so when I saw him first. I told mamma that there was something here——" She put her hand to her lips, and the tears filled her eyes. "We lost our dear father all in one moment," she said; "thus we know what it is to be unquiet. But at least you are warned. You can watch over him, and many times that goes on for a long time."

"Oh, there is nothing the matter—I mean papa is not ill," cried Helen, half alarmed, half amazed. "At least, it is only——"

"That is what we said," said Cécile gently; "it is only—a little want of breath, a little palpitation. And we might have taken more care perhaps to avoid emotion—to avoid danger; but who can say? *Le bon Dieu* knows best."

"I assure you," said Helen, "I am not alarmed at all about papa. We are not so well off as we were, and he wishes to be quiet, that is all. I think he likes Latour, and I like it. Yes, I think we shall stay all the winter. Perhaps we shall stay always. Janey will not remember any other place."

"But you—were you not sorry to leave your home?"

"Sorry?" said Helen, meditating. "I ought to have been. I do not quite know, it was so strange. Before I knew that we had left home we were here, or, at all events, at Sainte-Barbe," she said, with a smile.

"Sainte-Barbe? that is a long way off, beyond Dijon. But tell me, is it not very gloomy in England, more gloomy than here? Thérèse was quite right, I am *fiancée*, and I shall live in England. Tell me a little about your home."

"I was thinking of it when I saw you," said Helen. "Little Janey said the snow was like a great white cake—like the cake we had on Twelfth Night, and that made me think. I thought I saw the room all dressed with holly—we do that in England at Christmas; and all the children from all the parish —they came from miles round—and the great huge cake. The children all came and curtseyed to us when they had their slice of cake, and stared at Janey. She looked like a little fairy princess," said Helen, with a smile and a sigh. Her new acquaintance looked at her

very closely, then gave a glance at the child, who was very simply dressed, not like a princess at all.

"The people loved you very much?" said Cécile; "they do so in England; they do not hate you as aristocrats. I shall be very glad of that. Why should they hate us in France? We try to do what good we can, but there is always suspicion. They think we have no right to differ from them. But how can we help it? It is so, it is not our doing. They have not that feeling in England. They loved you, the people? Oh, how happy I shall be!"

"They were always very nice," said Helen. "Loved—I don't know that they loved us. We do not say that word in England except when—except when it is very strong indeed; —but they were always very nice. Though Miss Temple used to say papa was too good —a great deal too liberal, giving them too much—almost everything they wanted."

"Miss Temple was——?"

"My governess," said Helen—"my very dear friend—she went away from me and married. I never had a mother, nor Janey either," she said, in a low tone.

"But it was very good, very kind of Monsieur your father to be so good to the poor."

"I thought so too; but Miss Temple said it was wrong to give so much," said Helen simply. She did not understand the wonder that was rising in the mind of her new acquaintance. What Helen innocently revealed seemed to Cécile the condition of a grand seigneur in the old days when a grand seigneur was a prince in rural France. And it was very extraordinary to think of a great English nobleman or gentleman—words of which she partially understood the meaning —living in Latour! She looked at Helen again, examining her very closely; and Cécile knew that her dress, which was the dress she had brought from Fareham, was costly and fine, though so simple. They had wondered, gazed at the English family in church, and wherever they met them. But it was still more extraordinary now. The only thing was that they were English. That accounts for so much! for every kind of eccentricity, Cécile thought.

"Some friends, some people whom we know—indeed," said Cécile with pretty dignity, "why should I not say it?—the gentleman who is my *fiancé* is coming soon to see us. You will like to meet your compatriots? But I hope you will come before that time— oh, long before! as soon as you will—to-morrow! I should like to show you the

Château. It is very old and curious. You will forgive us for not going sooner to see you. We hoped mamma would have been well ; but now they tell us that she must not go out all the winter. She who loves the air so much and to be active. She will like to see you, Miss——"

"You promised to call me Helen." Helen had forgotten her own horror about the name, and said this with a mischievous sense of amusement, her pleasure in her new friend and in the prospect thus offered to her opening up all the closed doors in her heart. She laughed as she spoke. It had gone out of her mind that for the moment she had no name.

"It seems too familiar," said Cécile gravely, "for the first time ; but if it is so that in England one does not say miss—but they do say it, or why should the word exist?— I will willingly call you Helen. Do you thus pronounce the 'h'? In France we say (H)élène."

"Is it that Mademoiselle will come to the Château to-morrow?" said Thérèse, coming up. "The little one will come. She has told me a great many things. Oh, how it is pleasant to have some one new to talk to! She is delicious," cried the young Frenchwoman. "And Mademoiselle, I hope she too finds it pleasant to have friends."

"We are to say Helen," said Cécile with her air of dignity. They had reached M. Goudron's house as she spoke, where he was standing with an old shawl wrapped about his shoulders. He was not susceptible about his personal appearance. But the sight of Helen's companions made a change in his looks. He grinned, but he scowled as well. His countenance became diabolical between hatred and mockery. Thérèse caught her sister by the arm.

"He is like the demons in the pictures. I dare not go any nearer. Cécile, come! he will do thee some harm. Me, I am not *fiancé*, nothing is going to happen to me ; but he will bewitch thee, he will do thee harm."

"I am not afraid," said Cécile, though she trembled a little ; "there are no people in England who hate you because you are aristocrats, that makes me very happy. And you will come to-morrow to the Château? At one o'clock, after the *déjeuner*, will that do? and we will come to meet you. Then good-bye, à demain, au revoir," both the girls cried, turning hastily away. M. Goudron had put them to flight. The frown disappeared from his face as they turned, and the grin became more diabolical than ever.

"What a pity," he said, "Mesdemoiselles, that your fine friends, those magnificent young ladies from the Château, the young princesses, the great personages, should run away from a poor old man."

Little Janey had no restraints of politeness upon her. She pulled at the end of his eccentric old tartan shawl. "C'est parce que vous êtes si méchant," she cried. "C'est parce que you are a fright, a horrible, nasty, old man. I hate you too," cried Janey— "vous êtes méchant, méchant! Personne vous aime ; vous êtes, an old, old, wicked! a horror! a fright! all wrapped in a shawl like an old *vieille fille;* nobody loves you, they all hate you," she cried.

M. Goudron was dismayed by this sudden attack, and he had a weakness—he loved children. He cried in a querulous tone, "Petite, vous n'en savez rien," loudly, as if defying the world. At the window up-stairs Blanchette and Ursule were secretly kissing the tips of their fingers, waving anxious salutations to the departing ladies of the Château. As for Helen, she held her dress close to her, not to touch him as she brushed past into her own room. She was not so outspoken as Janey, neither did she think, like her father, that these extraordinary antipathies and political extravagances were fictitious like the politics of a vaudeville. But the horror was evanescent, and how delightful was the reflection that she had found a pair of friends !

CHAPTER X.

AFTER this a new life began for Helen. Cécile and Thérèse de Vieux - bois were much more highly educated than she was ; they were far more fluent in conversation ; they knew a great deal more than Helen. She, poor, solitary child, in her luxurious rural palace, had read nothing but novels ; whereas they had read scarcely any novels at all, but a great many better things, and still continued their studies with a conscientiousness and energy at which she gazed with wonder. Nothing could have been more different from their carefully guarded and sedulously instructed life than the secluded existence of the millionaire's daughter, broken sometimes by the noisy brilliancy of a great dinner party, at which, perhaps, she and her governess were the only ladies present, or by the arrival of the huge box of light literature which her father substituted when she was seventeen for the cakes and toys, and dainties of all kinds, with which he had overwhelmed her at an earlier age.

This was Mr. Goulburn's idea of what was best for girls—cakes and sweetmeats, then novels, with as many balls and amusements as could be procured. He had intended that Helen should be fully supplied with these later pleasures; but he had not succeeded, as has been said, in introducing her to the county, and all his plans for town had been mysteriously cut short. But the Count de Vieux-bois had gone upon a very different plan; and it is quite possible that just as Helen found it much more life-like and real to mend Janey's frocks and teach her her letters, so the Demoiselles Cécile and Thérèse might have found more satisfaction in the abortive balls and dinner parties, which might not have come to nothing in their hands. But the life of which Helen became a spectator at the Château filled her with admiration and awe. She could only look with respectful alarm at the volumes which the others worked steadily through, morning after morning, with the most noble devotion. No one so much as saw the young ladies at the Château till twelve o'clock, when the big bell rang, and they all came out of their rooms to the first common meal. " When do you work?" Cécile had said almost severely when Helen told her of the breakfasts in England. " If it is so I shall not like that at all. When can one work?—and if one does not read, and read much, how shall one be a companion to one's husband?" the young lady asked with great gravity. We have already said that domestic virtue and duty is, in France, for the time being, the highest fashion, the finest *cachet* of supreme aristocracy. Helen made the most simple, but, to this highly educated young Frenchwoman, the most bewildering reply. " Oh ! perhaps he will not read very much either. Gentlemen never do; they read the *Times* and the *Field*—and ; have I said anything wrong?"

(" Elle est folle donc," said Thérèse to Cécile. " C'est que son père est un homme de *sport*," said Cécile in an undertone to Thérèse.)

" You deceive yourself, chère Hélène," said the elder sister with a smile. " The journals are nothing; one must know what is going on. But if you knew how difficult it is to keep up with the reading of gentlemen—our dear father, for example. Mamma did not try. She said, 'It is useless at my age. I cannot do it; my daughters, I leave it to you.' And we tried, but never succeeded. Nevertheless, papa was very kind. He always recognised that there were diffi-

culties. But I am resolved to be a companion to my husband. I will not leave it to my daughters," said Cécile. " I have read your great writers, and a great deal of the constitutional history. And now I shall be ready to take up anything that John is doing."

" Is his name John?" said Helen with rising interest.

" It is a very pretty name," said Cécile ; " there are a great many in England. It is something like our Jean in France, but more *distingué*."

" Oh, much, much more distinguished," said Thérèse.

" He had not any title at first,' Cécile continued. " They say that in England that, too, is more distinguished. I thought I should be mistress. It is droll."

" We do not say mistress in England," said Helen. " Is he in the law, or in the Church, or a merchant, or only a gentleman ? Papa was a very great, great merchant," she continued, her cheeks colouring warmly. Though she was very quiet and gentle, yet in some things Helen had her pride too.

" And what is it to be only a djentleman ?" Thérèse said.

" That is when you *quite* belong to the county," said Helen—" when you have been always there, when the estate goes from father to son. There was a gentleman near Fareham, where we lived, a gentleman called Rashleigh——"

" I have heard those names," said Cécile with a little cry. " John has talked to me— I am sure I have heard them."

A mischievous light glanced over Thérèse's face. She made a sign to her sister. " All the names in England resemble each other. Tu te trompes, Cécile. And here is mamma."

The entrance of Madame la Comtesse put a stop to all the chatter. She talked herself steadily without intermission. She was a handsome, middle-aged woman, threatened, as she told everybody, with a *bronchite*. " I who never had so much as a cold in my life !" The talk of the girls was extinguished as tapers are extinguished in the light of the day, by the conversation of their mother. She spoke a little English badly, but a great deal of French very well.

" So Monsieur your father is ill, Mademoi-selle. I am grieved to hear it. Where there is but one parent, it is then that life becomes precious; though even *sans cela*—— Do not send for the doctor here; it is a good-for-nothing ; in medicine *bien entendu*, not in life. For his life, *mon Dieu !* I know nothing of it," the Comtesse said, shrugging her shoulders. "He is not of our *monde*. But Monsieur your father, Mademoiselle, you can do the most for him yourself. You can keep him from emotion; that is the great thing—from emotion. To do that, one must take a great deal of trouble, one must be always watchful; but for so dear a father one does not think of trouble. Were I allowed to go out I should see him; you should have the benefit of my experience; and, indeed, when he does me the honour to come here I shall spare no trouble; I shall observe him closely. It is my duty. I should be barbarous, I should not be Christian, did I not endeavour to be of use to you, so young, and a stranger."

"But, indeed, Madame!" cried Helen in despair, "my father——"

"I know what you would say," said the too sympathetic lady. "He will not allow that he is ill; it is what they all do. Ah me! to whom do you tell it? Have we not made the experience, my children and I? They are made like that; they will not be advised, they will not take care. Then the only thing, my child, is for you to take so much the more care. Let there be no emotion. That is the chief thing—no emotion. It would be well, perhaps, that you see his letters before they are given to him, and if any is of a character to cause excitement, keep it back. Ah, how much do I regret that I neglected some of these precautions! But, *mon enfant*, you must profit by our sorrow," said the Comtesse with tears in her eyes.

These advices were addressed to her continually, altogether unaltered by the fact that Helen protested, whenever she had a moment given her in which she could do so, against the supposed illness they had attributed to her father. She protested that he was not ill; but it made no difference. The Comtesse paid no attention, but entered with enthusiasm into the minutiæ of care-taking, recollecting now one thing, now another, that Helen could do—"Surtout point d'émotion!" They were so sure they were right that she came at last to listen without any protestation. The Château gave Helen an altogether enlarged and widened life. She was there almost every day, leading them into the wintry woods, at which they shivered, but which Cécile boldly braved now and then, on the strong argument that in England, whether it was winter or summer, everybody went out; or sitting with them near the ugly stove which kept their rooms so warm, discoursing now and then in her turn about the

English life which, to them, was so unknown. Helen, to tell the truth, did not know very much more about it than the two admiring girls who, on this point, believed all that she said. But she collected all her broken reminiscences, and all that she had heard from Miss Temple, and even, it must be added, some things which she had found in her novels, to instruct the eager mind of Cécile in her new duties. That she would have to walk out every day, whether it rained or snowed or blew a tempest; that she would have to be fully dressed by nine o'clock, in no robe de chambre, however pretty, or *négligé* of loosely knotted hair, but point device, and ready to receive visitors; that she would have to carry puddings to the cottagers, and take a class in the Sunday-school, and that the people would adore her. All this Cécile received with unbounded faith; though she was much disturbed by the Sunday-school, which had not been in her programme.

"But they will know I am a Catholic," she said.

"All the ladies do it," said Helen with steady dogmatism; and the two girls looked at each other with a gasp of dismay, but could not doubt what was so unhesitatingly given forth. There was great trembling about these Sunday-schools, so unnecessarily and boldly introduced, and the Curé was consulted, and even the Vicaire, and Cécile herself wrote to the superior of the convent in which she had been brought up. The Comtesse was of opinion that John should be written to at once, and the thing declared impossible; but Cécile would not consent to this. He would not wish her to do anything against her conscience, she knew; but, nevertheless, her dutiful soul was troubled. Thus Helen had her revenge.

And thus the winter stole on. Mr. Goulburn was with difficulty persuaded to pay a visit at the Château, where he was very silent, and bowed and listened to all that Madame la Comtesse had to say. He did not protest at all, as Helen did. But he excused himself when it was proposed that he should go again. Excitement was bad for him, he said with a gravity that filled Helen with the utmost amazement; and when the evening of the weekly dinner party came Helen went with M. le Précepteur and his wife, making apologies for her father, which were received in very good part.

"He is right," said Madame la Comtesse, "excitement is the worst thing in the world for him. I am glad he perceives that it is necessary to guard against it."

All this confounded Helen, who did not know what to think. Was it true that her father was ill? Was there really anything to fear?

But he did not appear ill, or at all different from his usual condition. He began to get his pines cut at last, confiding the business to the husband of Margot, not to Antoine, with whom, nevertheless, he did not quarrel, employing him in various odd jobs with an impulse of liberality which was very unlike anything to be found in Latour. Mr. Goulburn could not forget the habits of a man through whose hands money had streamed in large floods, and who had never had time to be economical. He gave employment with a freedom unknown in the locality, where everybody looked a great many times even at a sou before spending it. He was a new species to the thrifty villagers. He went daily and superintended the wood-cutting, and enjoyed the walk, however cold it was, a thing equally incomprehensible to them; but he would not carry even his own overcoat, calling the first idle lad he could find to do it for him, and throwing him fifty centimes for work which was not worth one sou. He saw everything done to the 'long straight pine-trunks; and at last, early in the spring, concluded the whole little enterprise, which had given him much satisfaction. They had been sold to an agent who had been at Latour during the winter, and who was as much pleased with his bargain as Mr. Goulburn was with his. He came home one day holding in his hand the letter which had contained this agent's remittances. It was the first letter he had received for months— the first sign of communication with the world which lay outside of Latour. "I have set up in business," he said; "there is no saying what it may come to. It is a pity there are no shops; I should have bought something for you girls. I have been making money even out here. By-the-bye, it makes my heart beat. I am not framed for excitement, as your old Comtesse says."

"Do you always make money, papa?" said little Janey. "What do you do it with? I should like to make some nice new money, like the new sous Cécile gave me." She had forgotten all about other coinage, and now knew nothing but the sous.

"This time, you know, I made it in the wood," he said. "Don't you recollect the gold among the trees?"

"That was only sunshine," said Janey. "I see that often; but you cannot put it in your pocket. Did you dig till you came to it, papa? Was it in a big box or in a jar deep down under the trees? Margot says there is some there, if we knew where to find it. Will you show me how you got yours, papa?"

"No, no, my little girl," he said; "you shall never soil your pretty fingers with it. There will be plenty for my Janey when I am dead."

"I don't want to have plenty when you are dead!" cried the child. "I don't want to have anything when you are dead. I should like then to be dead too."

"No, no, my little love. No, no, my Janey; you will live long, and you will be happy, and you will be kind to the poor, and think sometimes of your old father." He had taken her on his knee, and now leaned his head upon hers. "You will never believe any harm of your father, my little girl. Whatever they say of him, you will always remember that he was very fond of you."

"You do not feel ill, papa?" cried Helen, alarmed; while Janey, not understanding, but frightened too, peered up in his face with a pair of widely opened eyes.

"I believe it is that old witch at the Château," he said, and laughed. "I must beware of excitement, you know. To dine in her company being too much for me, how should I be able to bear the maddening delight of making a few francs in Latour? It will go off presently," he added, setting Janey down from his knee. And so it did, to all appearance; there was nothing wonderful in it. But the profit he had made amused him beyond description. It did him good— or harm. It set him thinking of the outside world, and wondering what was going on there. A thirst for a newspaper suddenly came upon him. What were they doing in the world? And he himself, what had been done about him? Had he been allowed to drop without any attempt at pursuit? Had things not turned out so badly as he thought? When a man feels himself pursued, the sense of getting into a place of safety, a close cover, is sweet; but after the pleasure of the security has penetrated into every vein, what man is there who can refrain from poking his head out of the cover to look for his pursuers, and from feeling a kind of disappointment at their total disappearance? To hear them strutting about, poking at every bush, calling to each other, now here, now there, foiled yet pursuing, is more flattering, more consolatory to the fugitive. But there had been nothing of this in Mr. Goulburn's case; he had slipped through their fingers; and after he had been pleased for a long time, now he began to be almost disappointed—he wanted the excitement. He was tired of the too complete safety of his life.

That night there was great news at the Château. John was coming. The wedding was to be at Easter; but he could not remain so long without visiting his bride; and with him was coming a relation, a gentleman. "Listen, Hélène," said Cécile—"we have no secrets for you. This gentleman, Monsieur Charles, is *très comme il faut*. I cannot say it in English. What words are there in English that say all that? He is not very rich; but mamma seeks to marry Thérèse, and in every other respect he is everything we could desire. John has often spoken of it. He has been in India, like so many of your young Englishmen. But if Thérèse and he please to each other, why should he go back? John says that if some one who is clever, a true man of affairs, an Englishman, were to manage our woods, we should be twice more rich; and if he pleases to Thérèse! Hush! it is a little family arrangement; nothing is to be said of it. But we watch for the eventualities. You will open your English eyes, *chère petite*, and you will give me your opinion upon him for Thérèse."

Helen felt a little chill at her heart; she could not tell why. A Monsieur Charles who had been in India! No doubt there were hundreds of them in England. "But," she said—and probably in any case she would have objected, for she had begun to be very British since she lived in France— "but an Englishman does not understand family arrangements like this. Does he know that he is coming for Thérèse?"

"That is what we cannot tell. We know that the English are very peculiar—very strange in their ideas."

"I think it is the French who are strange in their ideas," said Helen, with all the fervour of English prejudice. She was almost pleased to think that if M. Charles was a party to any such arrangement he was not at all so *comme il faut* as Cécile thought. "A *right* Englishman would not do it. Come to be looked at, as if he were applying for a situation as a servant!" Helen said to herself indignantly, that these were not English ways. She did not enjoy the evening. She was not herself. She contradicted everybody, even Madame la Comtesse. What was the matter with her?

"*Tiens,*" said the Comtesse, "these English

are so droll; it does not please them to meet each other. We others, we love our compatriots. When you are in England it is a fête to see a Frenchman. But the English are different; they will not encounter each other if they can help it. You will see that Djohn will be equally discontented to hear that there is an English family at Latour." This appeared both to Cécile and Thérèse a very likely solution of the question.

But Helen went home displeased and uncomfortable — displeased with herself, for what did it matter to her if some Englishman whose very name she had never heard, should adapt himself to the special point in which French domestic arrangements are repugnant to the English mind? It was nothing to her. If he pleased Thérèse and Thérèse pleased him, and everybody else was pleased, what had Helen to do with it? But it is astonishing how determined we often are to annoy ourselves about things with which we have nothing to do. "No doubt it would be a most excellent arrangement," she said to herself with a smile, which she felt must be very much like a sneer. In England people would be very much surprised; but Latour was not England, and probably Monsieur Charles had learned different fashions in India, which was not England either. She wondered what sort of person he could be, impatiently disengaging from her mind the shadow that would thrust itself forward of the Monsieur Charles who had been in India, and who had also been in Sainte-Barbe. Whoever it might be, it could certainly not be he. And yet how he would thrust himself into her imagination, poke himself forward, with his light hair and sun-burned countenance! She wondered—if it should happen to be he after all—would Thérèse like him? and what would he think, to find her, Helen, established there? and would he look in the same way and speak in the same way as he had done at the Lion d'Or? "In what way?" she said to herself sternly, and herself replied, "Oh, in no way at all!" with an impatient fling of the head. It was lucky that her companions chattered all the way, for Helen made no addition to the conversation. And it was not a very long way. The Château had no lengthened avenue, no seclusion of lawns and trees between it and the village, but stood close to the road with patriarchal bareness and simplicity. It was a moonlight night, and the softening of spring was in the air. There was a little commotion, too, unusual to it, in Latour.

The young men of the village were about in groups, the *cabarets* were more full than was usual, except on Sundays. Helen recalled to herself with a little effort a thing in her pre-occupation she had forgotten. The next day was the day on which the lots were to be drawn for the conscription. Poor little Blanchette's heart was full of trembling, and there was many an ache of anxiety in the village. With all her homely neighbours in such suspense, to think that she should be able to make herself almost unhappy about this Monsieur Charles from beyond the sea!

CHAPTER XI.

HELEN had meant to go to mass on the morning of the day when the young men of the village were to draw for the conscription, but she was late, as the interested and distressed young spectator so often is at the critical moment. Ursule had gone to the early mass before break of day, and had stayed in church till the draw was over and the young conscripts coming out of the Mairie with their number, bad or good, in their caps. Madame Dupré would have liked to do the same, but she was afraid of the ridicule of her neighbours, who certainly would have taunted her with trying to curry favour with the *bon Dieu* at the moment when she was in need of His help. Not being able to do this, she began a special "cleaning out," such as, in all regions, is soothing to the female mind perturbed. As the moment approached, the poor woman grew more and more cross, snapping at every one who approached her. M. Goudron, who liked to watch a dramatic situation, came in about ten minutes before the *tirage* began. "My house is all upside-down!" he said with keen enjoyment. "Nobody can pay any attention. One is praying and the other weeping, instead of awaiting with placidity whatever may have happened. I say to myself, Madame Dupré is an *esprit fort*. She will consider that a man must have his coffee, were the skies to fall. That is a thing that girls cannot be taught. I tell that little fool Blanchette, 'If thou wilt take an example, look at his mother, our good neighbour of the Lion d'Or!'"

"If I were thou, Jean Goudron, I would hold my peace. I would not meddle with what concerns thee not," said Madame Dupré, pushing against him with her great broom in her hand.

"*Comment!* my coffee? Does not that concern me?" cried old Goudron, with his grin.

Madame Dupré made no reply. Her round face was red as the embers on the hearth. She swept the dust out of all the corners, knocking her brush against the wall, making a great noise, and sweeping everything towards him. He got a mouthful of this dust, which, as it had not been stirred for some time, was of a piquant kind, and coughed. "Suffocate me not, *ma bonne femme*," he said. "I have done thee no harm!"

"How can I tell that?" cried the poor mother, in a frenzy of suspense and passion. "How do I know that thou hast not thrown an ill lot on my boy? That little saint Ursule, thou hast done thy best to keep her from praying for us; and it is thou, and such as thou, that make us ashamed to pray for ourselves! Get thee out of my sight, with thy devil's grin! Thou shalt have no coffee here."

"Bravo!" cried old Goudron. "Because thy son has gone to *tirer*, the whole world must stand still. There must be some one, *n'est-ce pas*, to cheat the others, to put the good number into his hands? Yes, yes; there must be a *bon Dieu* wherever there's a woman!" said the old man. But he did not go much further, for suddenly, before he was aware, Madame Dupré and her vigorous broom were upon him. She did not condescend to strike or push, but taking the lean old sceptic at unawares, swept him forth like a piece of rubbish. "Va, canaille!" she said. Old Goudron sprawled and stumbled forth, saving himself only from a prostration on the threshold by grasping at the first prop that presented itself. The conscripts were beginning to appear in the street with cockades in their caps, singing and shouting. They stopped to give him a rude salutation. They were all safe; they had drawn good numbers; they were wild with joy. "Look at old Jean Goudron! he is *ivre-mort!* The *bonne mère* has swept him out of the house!" "Pauvre Mère Dupré," said one among them, with a sob of excitement. Madame Dupré recognised the meaning of his tone. She came out, her broom in her hand, a paleness stealing over the red in her cheeks, and leant against the lintel of her door. She did not see the old man scowling and grinning at her, though he stood close by, waiting for the event. All was mist and darkness to her, save one thing. In the middle of the street was a figure alone, walking down slowly, looking at no one. His step, the sight of his folded arms and bent head, the stumble he made now and then, as he came over the rough stones, were enough, without words. Her eyes, too, were full of the giddiness of the calamity. She could see nothing but figures moving confusedly; faces looking out of the houses on the different sides of the village street all peering at him. It was Baptiste, with the ribbons of the conscript hanging sadly over his ear, and a big 3 in the front of his cap.

Helen looked out from her window just as this sad sight appeared. She felt a pang of guilt, as if it had been her fault. Oh! why had she not gone to the early mass to pray that he might have a good number? It did not occur to Helen that some one else must then have got a bad one. She heard a rush down the stairs, and saw Blanchette rush out across the street and fling herself upon him.

Poor little Blanchette! poor dumb mother, not able even to cry! Their arms met about him, one on each side, as if to tear him out of the hold of fate.

It is terrible when a great calamity happens in the morning; there is such an endless day to realise it in, to turn it over, to see it in every possible light. Ursule came back almost immediately, following Baptiste, with her head bowed upon her breast. "You have heard, Mademoiselle?" she said with a sob. "The *bon Dieu* has not thought fit to hear our prayers. There has been a want of faith on our part, or some other has prayed more strongly than we. We must not complain, Mademoiselle, for if the *bon Dieu* heard us

always it would be very easy to be a Christian. But only for my Blanchette it breaks my heart. Oh! if I were one of the saints in heaven—God forgive me for making so bold —I could not, I would not refuse any one! I would not take a denial! But when you are praying and praying, and there is no answer, heaven seems so far away, Mademoiselle."

"And is there nothing more that can be done?" Helen said, dropping a few tears of sympathy.

"Yes, Mademoiselle, there is my coffee to make," said old Goudron, who made his appearance just then; "which is their duty, what they are put into this world for, these girls—not to say incantations nor make a fuss about young good-for-nothings like the

conscrit yonder. My coffee, *petite hypocrite!*" he cried, pushing before him the little shrinking figure. Helen felt her countenance flame.

"You are a wicked, horrible old man," she cried in English, to relieve her mind, "and I hate you! Come in, M. Goudron," she added, with an effort; "the coffee is made; come in and take it here."

"Mademoiselle is too good," said the old man, surprised; but he let Ursule go. Helen had been too late to help in the praying, but perhaps there might be something left which she could do. Mr. Goulburn was late. He had not yet come down-stairs; and Margot, though she too had run out to take part in the melancholy excitement, could be brought back more easily than poor little Blanchette. Helen heroically poured out a large basin of coffee for the odious old man, whose sneer made her shiver; and he was so little prepared for this attention that for the moment he was entirely subdued.

"Mademoiselle is very good to take so much trouble," he said. "The coffee is excellent. I have always been told that no one understood how to be comfortable like Messieurs the English. Comfort! it is even an English word!"

"We try to be good to each other—that is what makes us comfortable," said Helen, with youthful severity. The coffee was served in little round basins of thick and heavy white crockeryware, and M. Goudron broke down his bread into it, and ate it with a spoon, which disgusted the English girl much, chiefly because it was not her way of taking the morning meal.

"I perceive," said M. Goudron, "you think I am not good to my grandchildren, Mademoiselle—notwithstanding that I feed them and lodge them, and allow them to give me a great deal of trouble. They cost me more than any one would think. They are not young ladies like Mademoiselle. Why should not they go out into the world and gain their living like others? It is because I have a soft heart," the old man said with a grin. "They are old enough to gain their living, yet I keep them at home. Is not that much? What would you have me do more?"

Helen did not know what to say. "You will not let them do anything they want to do," she cried with hot partisanship; but she was aware that there was not much reasonableness in the complaint, and this took away precision from her tone.

"One of them wants—to marry M. Baptiste, who is not what I approve, who is not *rangé* nor serious, but a young good-for-nothing," said M. Goudron. "Fortunately, Mademoiselle, that is put out of the question by this morning's luck."

"Fortunately!" ("Janey," said Helen in English, "I cannot bear him much longer. He is horrible; he is disgusting; he is like the ogre in your fairy tale.") "Fortunately, M. Goudron! when they love one another! when they will break their hearts! when——"

"Ah, bah! Excuse me, Mademoiselle; you are young and romantic, like all the English ladies; but I am prudent. I think of Blanchette's real welfare; and Mademoiselle, who is Protestant, a religion of good sense, does not desire me, I hope, to bury Ursule alive in a convent. Pah!" said M. Goudron,

spitting on the floor in sign of his disgust, a proceeding which elicited a restrained shriek from his young hostess.

"Janey, call Margot, call Margot! I cannot put up with him any longer. No one ever does that in England," she said, turning away with a face of horror.

"Shut a girl up in a convent?" said M. Goudron. "No, you are a prudent people; you have too much good sense. A girl who can do all that is necessary in a little *ménage*—who can make the kitchen very well, and mend my clothes, and do all that is needed, and is cheaper than a servant;—to shut her up in a convent, where she will no longer be of use to any one—and with a *dot*, if you please! Were they to take her with nothing we might think of it. That is what Mademoiselle would wish me to do—to give one, with her dot, to the nuns and priests, whom I abhor; and to give another to Baptiste Dupré; and for myself to hire a servant who would gad about from morning to night and cost me as much as both put together! Is that what Mademoiselle would have me to do?"

Helen made no reply, for just then a hurried step had come in at the door, and a new tumult of anxiety, of emotion, seemed to pervade the house. There was a little pause and whispering outside, and then the door was thrown hurriedly open, and Blanchette came in, a fountain of tears.

"Oh, pardon, pardon, chère Mademoiselle! It is because I am so unhappy. I think I shall die of grief. Grandpapa! I am come to ask you upon my knees to have a little pity upon us. Oh, ma bonne, douce, gentille demoiselle, help me! perhaps he will hear you. He is so rich, it would be so easy to him to do it. Grandpapa, if you will help us I will be your slave, I will never complain any more; I will do anything; I will never ask to go out, nor for any toilette, nor for pleasure. Mon Dieu! he turns away his head! he will not even listen. Oh, mes chères demoiselles, help me! He is so rich—what would it do to him? He would never feel it. We should all be happy and pray to God for him—and he, he would never feel it at all!"

"How dare you say I am rich! Do not believe her, Mademoiselle; she is talking of things she knows nothing about. *Petite sotte!* you had better get up and go home, and think of your duty a little."

"Here is my duty, grandpère," said poor Blanchette, on her knees. "Oh, help me, help me, mes bonnes demoiselles! He does not care for God, nor for his children; but he cares for his *locataires*. If Baptiste goes away his mother will be ruined, and he will be lost to me, and I shall die. Oh, my poor Baptiste! he never was wicked, only foolish a little, like all the young men ; and he knows better, a great deal better now. Grandpapa, if you will only be kind, if you will do what we ask you, we will pray God for you on our knees every day, as Ursule does. Oh, Mademoiselle, Ursule is a saint ; she prays for him just the same as if he were the kindest; and so will I. And when you die, which cannot be long, for you are old, you will find the advantage—God will listen to you because you have listened to us. He will not remember the wicked things you have done, nor how hard you have been, nor——"

"This is something which is admirable," said the old man, grinning more horribly than ever. " Mademoiselle, my grand-daughter is of opinion that I am wicked, that I am hard, that I am old and will shortly die. Bien, très-bien ! It is to please me she says all these pretty things. Va, petite imbécile !" He put out his foot furiously to push the kneeling girl away.

But Janey, who had been standing by listening all this time in unwonted silence, looking on with very curious eyes, investigating the strange chapter in human affairs thus exhibited to her, stepped in to the rescue.

"You *are* old, M. Goudron," she said, "and you are not good. Papa is good, though he is old, but not you. He would do whatever I ask him. If you will not give Blanchette what she wants, I will ask papa, and he will do it for Janey ; and then what Ursule gets from God will be for papa, and not for you ; and all the village will say, ' Down with that old Père Goudron and Vive l'Anglais!' Nobody loves you, M. Goudron," continued Janey, "not one. You are a very bad old man; you never do anything that is kind. It would be better to be a wolf in the wood than you, for the wolf would not understand, and you hear me talking to you. And when you die, which can't be long, you will be made into an old cinder" (Janey said *tison*). "You are very like one now; I think you must feel the fire burning you already," cried Janey vindictively, "you are so dried up and withered and wrinkled and wicked. *Tiens*, Blanchette, do not ask him any more ; I will get it from papa."

Janey put out her hand majestically, interposing her small person between the old man whom she had denounced and poor Blanchette, who had risen to her feet and turned her large astonished eyes, full of tears, up-on the child. Janey, in her four feet of stature, towered over from them all, her pretty hair streaming back as on a breeze of indignation, her eyes blazing. No consideration of circumstances or possibilities affected Janey. She was sublime, for she was absolute, above all reasoning. And while Blanchette started to her feet, half in fear of her grandfather, half in wondering hope at the impulse of this little heroine, the old man, on his side, cowered and shrank before her. He had one humanity in him, he was fond of little children ; and Janey, the strange little foreign creature, exercised a kind of fascination over him. He tried to change his grin into a conciliatory smile.

"Tenez, tenez, ma petite demoiselle," he said with a broken sort of whimper in his voice; "do not speak to an old man so. When you ask me for something in your pretty little voice, I will do it. I am not wicked, as you say; it is they who are wicked, robbing me of everything. But you are a little angel. Naturally your papa will do whatever you ask him. He is a milord ; he is rich, very rich, like all the English ; and I too will do what you ask me, though I am not rich, but poor. But you must not say 'A bas père Goudron!'" cried the old man again with a whimper. He twisted all his lean person into a grimace of deprecating amiability, drawing his long legs under him, clasping his bony hands, putting his grotesque head on one side, while Janey stood impassive, disapproving, majestic, stretching out one small arm as a shield over Blanchette, who for her part, arrested in the very act of weeping, stood with her pretty lips apart, her eyes very widely opened, and the tears dropping down her cheeks.

Just then Mr. Goulburn was heard coming down-stairs. He was in good spirits this morning : first he was heard whistling a favourite tune, then he began to talk to Margot, who had come in and was sweeping loudly, knocking her broom into all the corners by way of blowing off her emotion, as poor Madame Dupré had done. "So poor Baptiste has drawn a bad number," they heard him say, and at the words Blanchette's half-arrested tears burst violently forth again.

"Oh, Monsieur," cried Margot, outside. " what good one can do when one is rich ! If the Père Goudron would but be charitable one time in his life, and give the money for a substitute ! Otherwise their hearts will be broken, and it will be ruin to the Mère Dupré."

"Ah, a substitute!" he said, while the little company within listened with breathless attention. Then there followed a bar or two of Mr. Goulburn's favourite air, and the renewed knocks against the wainscot of Margot's broom, and the step of the Englishman, lighter than usual, his daughter thought. Had he got good news? He pushed the door open, then stood surprised at the group he saw. "Ah!" he cried, "it is early to receive visitors, Helen." They all turned their eyes upon him, Blanchette putting her hands together instinctively. Two pairs of entreating feminine eyes caught Mr. Goulburn's first glance; then his own fixed upon the little central figure, whose looks were less entreating than commanding. "Why, little Janey, what have you got to do with this?" he said.

"Papa," said Janey, speaking in French —on the whole, she now spoke in French with more dignity than in English, her utterance in her native tongue being still made sweet to foolish parental ears by a few cherished baby errors—"papa, I have promised that you will give what old M. Goudron is too wicked to give—the money that Blanchette wants for Baptiste. She will tell you how much it is. I have said," said Janey with a falter in her small voice, for she began to feel the need of crying, being only six after

all—"I have said that my papa would give the money for Janey. I know, I know," she added, bursting into her native speech, "that you will dive it for Janey, papa."

Mr. Goulburn stood, looking much astonished, while this appeal was addressed to him. He looked at old Goudron, crumpled up in his chair with his deprecating look, and little Blanchette dissolved in tears, turning dim, imploring eyes upon him; and at Helen, who was old enough to know better, who ought to have put a stop to it. But he had not the habit of economy in money, and it did not occur to him, as it might have done to, alas! a better man, to consider a demand of this kind for a considerable sum out of mere kindness, to be at once out of the question. It was not out of the question to Mr. Goulburn. When a man's first quality is to be honourable and just above all things, he has to assume a sternness of self-restraint which sometimes makes him appear less amiable to superficial eyes; but one who is less decided upon such points is free of that bondage. He had spent money largely all his life, and he was not startled when he was asked for it, as most of us are who have to gain it by the sweat of our brow. He had never done much more than turn it over in his hands, gaining, yet sometimes losing, by chance, by luck, by hairbreadth hazards,

4

but never by the strain of daily toil ; and he had been in the habit of giving it away freely, whether it was his own or others', all his life. But he was somewhat annoyed by this demand. Helen should have done better. She knew that he was not now a millionaire, that his resources were limited. These hesitations made a cloud over his face when little Janey began to make her little speech. But suddenly the cloud rolled off in a moment, the light broke out. He had not a noble face ; a physiognomist would not have trusted it, an artist would have thought nothing of it ; there were ignoble lines in it, something which told of cunning, a furtive look—but all at once it was transfigured. He broke out into a half laugh, half sob—

"I oughtn't to do it ; I've no right to do it ! But I can't refuse to dive it to Janey!" he cried, with that clamour of mingled feeling in his voice, and drew the child triumphant into his arms.

How hoarse and broken the sound was ! Helen took fright. "Papa, you are ill !" she cried.

He went on laughing, not able to stop himself. "Not a bit," he said, sitting down and panting for breath. "Bonjour, M. Goudron ; you are a wise man, you are not led by the nose like me. Janey, my pet, tell your Blanchette to dry her eyes. We can't have any crying such a bright morning ; and let her send this conscrit to me."

"It would be better, a great deal better, for him to accept the lot he has drawn, and serve as he ought, and give up all follies," said old Goudron, gathering himself up out of his chair. He stood for a moment balancing himself on his long legs, somewhat crestfallen, yet recovering his grin. "I have to thank Mademoiselle for her excellent coffee," he said, "and her hospitality, truly English. Tenez, Mademoiselle la petite ; you will say au revoir before I go?"

Janey put her two hands behind her, and fixed him with two glittering eyes. "I am afraid I shall see you again, but I wish I never might," she cried. "You are a bad, bad, *horrible* old man !"

"And you, you are a charmante petite demoiselle," said M. Goudron, grinning at her till his old face seemed cut in two.

CHAPTER XII.

THE day of the *tirage au sort* was not one which could be spent like other days, after the supreme excitement of the morning. There was a great deal of wine consumed in Latour, and a perfect Babel of talk. It soon became known in the village, after a great many excited communications between the Lion d'Or and M. Goudron's house, that l'Anglais had offered to procure a substitute for Baptiste. At first the little eager world was incredulous of such an extraordinary announcement. L'Anglais ! a stranger, one who had nothing to do with the Duprés or the Goudrons, or even with the district, or any interest in the Lion d'Or ! but it was very evident that something was going on in which the stranger and Baptiste and Blanchette and all their respective families were involved. Madame Dupré, who had been assisted to her room by a whole assembly of weeping and sympathetic neighbours, had been disinterred from the midst of them and conducted across the street by Baptiste, very solemn and pale, yet with an expression quite different from the despair on his face when he had come home from the Mairie with his fatal number. It was Blanchette who, laughing, crying, with the tears on her cheeks and a voice broken with sobs, yet an extraordinary gleam of happiness about her, had flown across the light street, as a bird, to call them. They had all disappeared into the rooms on the ground floor, where there had been a tumult of talking and crying, two or three voices audible together, a thing never heard before since the English family, who spoke, the Latourois thought, almost in whispers, had taken possession. And then the Curé had been sent for ; and M. le Maire himself, coming home after presiding officially over the business of the day, still with his scarf on, and in all the pride of office, had stepped in. This diverted the attention of many from the noisy youths who had escaped, and who were celebrating their freedom, and from those who had been drawn, and who were trying to forget it and drown their despair. And when Madame Dupré came back, a changed woman, her head high, her countenance radiant, the whole community was stirred. It was true then ? Many were the wistful women who crossed the road after, and hung about the door, and cast anxious looks at the window. Why should Baptiste Dupré be the only one to be delivered? L'Anglais probably did it out of mere eccentricity, they thought, not out of regard to Baptiste, and no doubt he was enormously rich, and did not know what to do with his money ; and if he bought back Baptiste, why not Jean and Pierre? The mothers of Jean and Pierre, who had drawn the numbers 2 and 4, could not see the difference. They hung about the door all the day, thinking if he would but appear they might find courage to speak to him. The lucky Baptiste to have caught his attention! M. Goudron himself was not visible. He did not stand at the door and grin as he was in the habit of doing. The commotion had subdued him at least, and if there had been nothing else for which to thank l'Anglais, this was something, for these poor women, with their hearts full, felt that they could not have borne Père Goudron's grin. And soon it became whispered in the crowd that it was Antoine who was going to accept Baptiste's place. He had served already, being so much older, and most people were very glad to hear that he was going out of Latour. It would be so much the better for the other young men. Antoine had announced himself as ready to be any one's *remplaçant*: things had been going badly with him all the winter, and the money tempted him. There had been great bargainings in the room where so much unusual talking had been going on and so many people crowded together, and at last, by the help of the Maire and Curé and old Père Goudron himself—who, now that nobody expected him to supply the funds, could not keep himself out of the negotiations—Antoine consented to take fifteen hundred francs as the price of his service. He was giving himself, as he declared, "dirt-cheap;" but as Mr. Goulburn, though he was so liberal, had his wits about him, and old Goudron was the keenest at a bargain in all Burgundy, the whole preliminaries were arranged the same morning, and the money was to be paid as soon as possible. "For we are birds of passage," the Englishman said, "there is no knowing how long we may stay." That same night, no later, all guarantees having been given, Antoine was to get his price; and thus, after thanks and blessings innumerable, the scene ended. It was a relief to them all when the outpourings of gratitude were over and all those effusive people gone. "In England they would have felt it just as much, but they would not have made such a fuss," Mr. Goulburn said with a sigh of relief.

"You could not have done it in England," said Helen. "I think it is very good of you to do it, papa."

He looked at her with a smile on his face. "Do you know, I think so too—it was very good of me. But it was all for Janey," he said; "it will come off her fortune. I have got her fortune laid by all safe. I don't speak of yours, Helen, for you know you have something from your mother. You have a hundred a year, and as it has always been

left untouched to accumulate, there should be a good deal more than a hundred a year now. It is as well you should know, in case of——"

"In case of what, papa? You said we were birds of passage. Did you mean anything? Did you—think we might have to go away?"

"Not I! I don't know why I said it. The fact is we *are* birds of passage. What have we to do here? I am very comfortable; I don't want to change; but as a matter of fact things might happen——"

"Papa, perhaps I ought to have told you; they are expecting visitors—English visitors—at the Château."

She looked at him after a moment, and gave a sudden cry of alarm. He had become not pale, which is one thing, but white to the very lips. "Do you know who they are?" he said.

"Only their Christian names: one is John and the other Monsieur Charles, who has been in India."

She said this with an uneasy feeling once more that M. Charles who had been in India could be but one person, and looked up with some anxiety to see if her father would take the same view.

"That does not tell very much," he said with a laugh; "most men who are not called John are called Charles. Are they brothers? It is annoying. I dare say you wonder why I should care; but the fact is, Helen," he said with an uneasy attempt at a careless manner, "I don't want to come in contact with Englishmen. Take care not to mention my name at all; ignore me, that is the best thing to do. I won't meet any Englishman. I'd rather, a great deal rather, notwithstanding that things suit me very well here, go away at once than have English visitors prying upon me."

"I am afraid you are not well, papa."

"It is that old Comtesse that has put it into my head. There never was anything so absurd. I have been quite breathless and queer ever since she told me I ought to be so. It is the most droll sympathetic sensation—nothing more. I know I am not ill, not a bit ill—but I feel it; in the face of my own reason and all the facts of the case. Never mind, that will all blow off. And Helen, recollect what I say: be on your guard if you see any Englishmen. Stop; if it should by any chance be some one we know——"

"That is so unlikely, papa," said Helen, forcing herself to smile. But she did not think it was improbable, in her heart.

"It is very improbable; still we must be

prepared for all that can happen. Should it be any one we know, say that we have come here—for a day or two. Say that we are —just leaving—or better, say that you are alone, and that where I am you do not know."

It was Helen's turn now to be pale. "Papa, how can I say all these things?" she cried. "If I could, if the truth did not matter, the Vieux-bois would know I was lying. And, papa! oh, if you would but tell me! If it was only that you were ruined, why should you be afraid of English visitors? I think I could bear it better if you would tell me the truth. Is it only—what you call ruin, papa? meaning that you have lost your money?" she said.

"It is only—ruin. That is a tolerably big word. I don't know what you could wish more."

"But meaning that you have lost your money? You have not lost all your money," she said with some vehemence. "You have given—a great deal, to poor Baptiste. We are in no want of anything. You cannot have lost it all—that is not true."

A dull sort of smile came upon his face. "Such things happen every day," he said; "a man may lose all his money and may yet have what will do to go on with. Besides, it is Janey's, not mine."

Helen looked at him with such wistful wonder, with such a pained entreaty in her face, that he went on with an embarrassed laugh, "The short and the long of it, if you will know, is this—Ruin means not starva- tion, as you may suppose, but owing money which you cannot pay."

A hopeful gleam flew across her face. "But then, so long as there is any we can always go on paying. Ah, poor Baptiste! it would be hard to take it from him now; try anything else, papa; you shall have mine if you like, and welcome. And perhaps they would take it in instalments, as the poor people used to do at the Fareham Club."

"Hush!" he said, "you don't understand anything about it. I want no more conversa- tion on this subject."

"But, papa, I do understand: what can be more simple? Take the money we have, and pay as far as it will go, and then we could go home."

"You are a little fool," Mr. Goulburn said.

Helen was pained. Did she not under- stand? and yet it seemed so entirely simple. She did not insist any more, feeling that her father looked ill; that it was unkind to press

him for the moment. "If any of the people to whom he owes money should come here," she said to herself, "I should know what to do." It was with this feeling she set out. Janey was in the garden with Margot's children perfectly happy; her sister was not sorry on this day of emotion to be alone. She walked away quickly to the Château, and her story about the drawing and those upon whom the bad numbers had fallen was full of interest for the ladies; they wanted to hear every name, and how the unfortunates had borne it.

"Pierre Courvoye! oh, it will not do any harm to Pierre; and I think a few years' steady service and discipline will be of use to Jean too."

"But poor old Elisabeth," cried Cécile.

"She will be better without him; at least she will not see him going wrong; and per- haps he will do better in the regiment."

"But Baptiste? it will ruin Baptiste and poor Mère Dupré, and break little Blan- chette's heart," the girls cried.

When they heard that Mr. Goulburn had bought him a substitute there were no bounds to their enthusiasm. "Your papa then is a saint, he is a benefactor, he has a heart of gold," they cried.

"But, mon enfant," said the Comtesse, "I fear you must have allowed him to be ex- posed to emotion. Never forget that there must be no emotion; you must avoid it as you would avoid poison."

This flutter of interest and kind, pleasant talk and praise sent all that was melancholy out of Helen's head. She was to return home early, but this was the evening of Madame la Comtesse's dinner, and they were all to meet then. "Shall I tell her?" whis- pered Cécile.

"Oh, no, no; let it be a surprise," cried the more mischievous Thérèse. They went out with her to show her how all the young larches were pushing out their tassels, and the crocuses coming up by hundreds in the grass. Helen returned to the village by the longer way. There was a grand entrance to the Château which was scarcely ever used; a short avenue with two curious tall bits of building on either side of the gate, half towers, half houses, three stories high, giving a half- ludicrous air of defence in the midst of a line of low and innocent hedges. When im- portant visitors came this was how they went in; and, as it happened, she had scarcely emerged from between the two obelisks of houses which blocked the gateway, when she saw the Comtesse's great lumbering old family

coach, the "berline," as they called it, sway-ing along the road, drawn by the two long-tailed horses from the farm, with old Léon on the box, who was called Monsieur l'Inten-dant in the village when the people wanted to please him. Helen's heart began to beat. She felt sure that the occupants of the berline must be the English strangers whom she looked for with so much expecta-tion, yet fear. She gave a hurried glance at them as they lumbered past. She saw two heads, but her eyes were hazy with over-anxiety, and her excitement confused her. She could not tell who they were, or if she had seen them before. The carriage passed her. She breathed more freely. How foolish! she said to herself. Was she disappointed that after all it was not Charley Ashton? or was she relieved? or what was it? She could not tell. Her life had been full of a vague expectation, which had gone to her head, which had kept her amused, excited, disturbed, alive to everything. And now it had failed. Was not she glad? She ought to have been; it would keep safe her father's secret, and save him from all disturbance. But Helen's first sensation was as if she had fallen out of the clouds. The earth is a very steady, very satisfactory thing to come down upon, and by far the safest footing, but still when you drop from a height there is apt to be a momentary jar.

She was so full of this really involuntary, unwilling sensation, and so anxious to feel glad that all cause for apprehension on her father's part was over, that she did not hear the much louder jarring and grinding of the wheels with which the big berline, as soon as it had passed her, was stopped. Helen felt slightly unsteady so far as she herself was concerned. Her steps wavered; there was a ringing in her ears. It had been, she said to herself, something to look forward to, and it was over; and she was very glad it was over, and papa happily escaped from all annoyance. Things were getting steadier before her eyes every moment, her step was getting more assured. Then all at once she heard voices in the air. "I certainly will not wait for you," in a somewhat severe tone, and in familiar English accents.

"Never mind, you will just have time for your own salutations, and I will follow directly," some one said.

Helen's feet, in spite of her, swerved, stumbled, took her halfway across the road, like feet that were drunken and beyond guid-ance. She had not been mistaken after all. Whatever was to come of it, had she not known it all from the very first? She was not surprised now, though the discovery set her heart beating once more as if it would break out of her breast. Of course it was he. Could anything be more precise than the description, M. Charles who had been in India? She had been quite sure of it all along.

"Once more I have to ask, is it you, Miss Goulburn? I am sure it can be no one but you."

"Yes, it is me," said Helen simply (but nobody pretends that grammar and nature are the same in respect to this pronoun. She was much disturbed, and she could no more have said I than she could have flown); "and I thought it must be you they meant," she added, with more simplicity still, " though I heard nothing but your Christian name."

"Who was it that spoke of me? It is only by accident I have come here. I was going to Sainte-Barbe to find out if anything had been heard of you—if I could find any trace of you."

"Sainte-Barbe! we left that, Mr. Ashton, immediately——"

"I know: after you had seen me."

Helen sighed. It seemed impossible to her to lie as her father had told her—to say anything to him that was not true. It was very hard even to say what she did falteringly, "We did not mean to stay there, anyhow."

"Miss Goulburn," he said, "I have heard a great deal since I knew you have been home. When I saw you last I knew nothing. Miss Temple—I mean my stepmother—is very, very anxious about you. She wants you to go and live with her, and my father wishes it too."

"Mr. Charles, that is very, very kind," said Helen, shaking her head.

"Miss Goulburn, nobody in the world can take more interest in you, can have thought more of you than I, since you were a little girl at the school feasts. And in India I always wondered how you had grown up—if I should still find you when I got back. I don't know if you are aware of all that has happened?"

"Papa is ruined," said Helen in a very low voice.

"Ruined! ah, yes; and something more."

Helen trembled, tottering along by his side. "I asked him to tell me, but he wouldn't. Don't tell me, I had rather not know. Most likely," she said, with a thrill of much pain in her voice, "when he knows you are here he will go away."

"I am almost sure he will. And you have friends here."

"Oh, yes; all the people are our friends, every one. But what does that matter?" cried Helen with a smile of desperation. "It need not make any difference. We shall go all the same. We shall not mind. But why

you or any one should want to harm us, Mr. Charles, I cannot tell. We never did harm to any one. Why should we have to fly from one place to another? We have done nobody any harm."

Young Ashton looked at her with the tenderest pity in his face. "I came," he said, "to take you home, if you would come, if I could find you, to Mrs. Ashton. Every effort has been made to find you. We did not know what to wish—that he might not be found, or that you might. Pardon me, it was for this I came."

"Oh, no; for a very, very different purpose, Mr. Ashton! I know that quite well—I know exactly," said Helen with a little heat. Then she stopped confused. What had she to do with it? Whatever he came for, what was it to Helen? Angry! was she angry? But for what, in the name of heaven? Then she was angry with herself for her irritation. The tears gathered thick in her eyes. "It will be better, much better, to let us alone," she said; "what does it matter to any one where we go, or where we stay? Never mind us, please. Go to the Château, where they expect you. You can say I will not come this evening; you need not say why. And let us alone, Mr. Ashton. What can it matter to you if we are here or anywhere else? We have done no harm to you."

"Miss Goulburn, you don't know John; but he has been a sufferer; he is very bitter, he will not let things alone. If I could have formed the least idea that you were here—but even if I had known, what could I do to keep him from the place where his bride is living? And if he has any suspicion he will not be silenced. When I saw you—you with your open, candid face—walking so quietly along the road, and he by my side with the spirit of a bloodhound in him—— And yet how glad I am that you are here. But your father; good heavens!" cried the young man, "what a position for you to be in; you, so young, so innocent, knowing nothing!"

Just then they were met by a party of country people going home. "Bon soir, Mademoiselle," they cried with a little acclamation of kindness, the men taking off their hats; and one old woman paused to say, "You should be happy to-night if any one should, ma bonne demoiselle."

"You have been doing something kind," said young Ashton, looking at her, his face full of tender admiration and sympathy.

"Not I, not I," Helen cried. The tears came down her cheeks in a torrent. "It is papa, poor papa, that has been kind. You don't know how good he is. He has made some of the poor people very happy; and his reward," she cried, "will be to be driven away. Oh, why should that be? Papa, who used to be so rich, who had everything; and now that he is quiet here, in a little wretched village, you come and drive him away!"

Young Ashton's countenance changed. It grew grave, almost severe. "I do not drive him away," he said. "If there was anything I could do to make him safe, I would do it; but he will know better than you do that I cannot. Tell him that Sir John Harvey is here. He will understand that better than anything. Not in search of him—not knowingly, but still he is here. Do they know at the Château? Can they give any information? Will they put John on the scent? Pardon me for using such words—he is my cousin, but he is a hard man. Do they know who you are?"

Helen drooped her head with a bitter sense of shame. Even now she did not know what the real stigma was; but the shame of a false name bowed her to the ground. "They do not know us," she said almost inaudibly, "by our true name."

And as she stood before him with her head bent down and that flush of humiliation on her face, Ashton's heart was too full to keep silence. A cry of painful sympathy came from his lips. He took her hand and kissed it with passionate sympathy and anguish. "My poor child, my poor child!" he cried. "You, you! to have this burden to bear. Leave him, for God's sake, and let me take you home."

"Leave him! now, when he is badly off and in trouble?" This idea brought a kind of smile to Helen's lips. "But, Mr. Ashton, I think you mean very kindly. I will tell him, and you can say to them at the Château that he was not very well, that the excitement had told upon him, and that I could not leave him to-night. They will understand that. And don't make them think any harm of us, not more harm than you can help. They have been very sweet to me," Helen said after a pause, her tears dropping again; "such friends! and Thérèse, Mr. Ashton, Thérèse, remember! She is not Cécile, but she is nearly as good as Cécile."

"I know nothing about Thérèse or Cécile," he cried. "Helen, oh, forgive me, I am almost mad! Are you to be swept away from me once more? am I to lose you again?"

She shook her head sadly. "What does it matter? we never did know each other much," she said.

"I will come to the village after it is dark. I will wait about on the chance of seeing you; perhaps even I might be of use. Don't refuse me this," he cried; "don't refuse me so much as this! If it is I that must drive my own happiness away, at least let me see you once again."

"Yes; it is true, if you are a friend, you might be of use. You might help me, perhaps," Helen said simply, "if you will be so kind. That is the house, that tall one with the green shutters. It will be very kind if you will come."

She turned away, making a gesture to him to go back. They were opposite the Lion d'Or, where still the conscrits were hanging about with their coloured ribbons, and Baptiste receiving once again perpetual congratulation. Antoine, with his hands in his pockets, strolled along in the middle of the street, biting a straw which he held in his mouth. He was looking at M. Goudron's windows with bended brows. Amid all the peaceful surroundings, he alone caught Charley Ashton's eyes as a sinister figure meaning mischief; but he was far too much occupied with other thoughts to waste any upon the village bully at a moment so full of heavier trouble and pain.

CHAPTER XIII.

HELEN went home with slow steps and a heavy heart.

A heavy heart, indeed; it had beaten wildly enough within the last hour—now it lay in her breast like a lump of lead. This morning, though there was nothing happy in her own position; though she knew that some great cloud of misery and doubt hung between them and everything they had hitherto known, and that even the tranquillity of the moment, such as it was, might be interrupted in a second, in the twinkling of an eye; yet the triumphant lightheartedness of youth had been able to triumph over all these things. And there had been so warm an atmosphere of life about them, so much interchange of feeling, keen sympathy, and the profound happiness of making others happy, that very little sense of being there as a stranger had remained in Helen's mind. They were not strangers—they were more at home in Latour than they had ever been in Fareham. Here everybody knew them, everybody had a friendly word for them; more than that, the English family, with its careless, liberal ways, had now secured the affection of the village. She herself had never known before what it was to have friends like Cécile and Thérèse,

or to be interested with such familiar kindness in any poor girl as she had been in the
fortunes of little Blanchette. At Fareham the
love of the village publican's son with the
retired tradesman's daughter would have been
nothing to the great young lady, secluded
among her woods and parks. But here they
were more interesting, and concerned her
more than any romance. She had a share in
the lives of so many people, and her own life
was full of tranquil occupations, of sympathies, of friendships; every cottage round
about contained something or somebody that
interested her. But what of that? They must
all be left behind, as all her other habits of
living, all her previous existence had been.
She would have to give up those first personal friends, not knowing if she should ever
see them more, not hoping to do so—and go
away from the homely little life which had
given her her first lively sense of individual
existence—for what? to go where? Helen
could not tell. The world was all dark beyond this one clear spot in which the afternoon sun had just sunk behind the cottage
roofs, and the whole sky overhead was red
with gorgeous reflection. To-morrow, the
fine spring morning which these ruddy lights

prophesied, would rise serenely over the same
roofs, and Margot would light her fire, and
little Blanchette, out of her dreams, would
awake joyfully to recollect that her troubles
were all over. But where would Helen be?
She did not know, but surely away from
Latour, away from everything she knew, out
into the world, which always figured itself
before her as darkness—the gloom of night,
the clanging of a great train, pursuing its
noisy precipitate way through an unseen
country, to the unknown out of the known.
She stood for a moment at the door, looking wistfully round her at the familiar scene.
The houses with their thatched roofs rose
dark against the great glow of redness in
the west. In the distance the homely spire
of the church rose up protecting over them;
voices were in the air, all cheerful, confused,
half heard, with now and then one distincter
note striking in, as by turns one figure
would start up and separate itself from the
little company still lingering in front of the
Lion d'Or. Somewhere near a woman was
singing a baby to sleep, in a sweet drowsy
voice, broken by the rock of her chair upon
the wooden floor. On the other hand a
group of little truants, pattering in their sabots,

were being pursued homewards to bed by the half-laughing, half-angry mother. Helen looked round her with wistful eyes, casting a last glance along the road which led to the Château, the most dear of all. Along this road Antoine was sauntering slowly, his hands in his pockets, looking back as he went, with his eyes always fixed on M. Goudron's house. His was the only non-sympathetic figure in all the scene. It broke the spell. Helen turned from him and breathed her farewell to the village in one long sigh.

The prattle of Janey was the first thing she heard when she went in. The child was seated on her father's knee. She had been telling him a story about Margot's children, with whom she had been playing.

"Petit-Jean does not know what a big city is, papa; he thinks Paris is like Laroche" (Laroche was the next village, and had a street twice as long as that of Latour, and was looked upon as almost a *chef-lieu*). "He said, was England like the little island in the pond at the Château? Margot's little children they are very ignorant, they don't know anything, papa."

"And my little Janey knows a great deal?" he said laughing, yet with a thrill of another sentiment in his voice; "but everybody, my pet, has not travelled like you."

"No," said Janey complacently. "Only think, I came from India when I was a little tiny baby—if I could only recollect I should know India too, and then London, and then that place on the sea where we bought our things, and then Sainte-Barbe, and then—— Papa, after all this, when are we doing home?"

"Should you like to do home, Janey?" This time the laugh was so broken that it was more like a sob.

"Oh, yes, papa. I should like to have my big doll Marianna, that I put in my bed when we came away. Will she always be in my little bed all this time, staring with her big eyes? I forgot to shut her eyes when I put her in. Fancy a little girl lying for years and years with open eyes!"

"It is not years and years, Janey."

"Yes, papa, it is longer, longer than any one can remember—far longer than *that*," cried the child, stretching her arms to the widest. "I want to do home."

"Here is Helen coming to put you to bed," he said. She was in his arms as she sat there, but he strained her closer, kissing her little upturned face again and again. "My little Janey, my little darling," he said, "wherever you are you will not forget your poor father, who was so fond of you?"

She did not take much notice of this address, being used, more or less, to speeches of the sort, but slid down from his knee. Helen had to postpone her explanation till the ceremony of putting the child to bed was over. Should she be obliged to wake her up again in the dark as had been done before? And how would it be possible here, thirty miles from the railway, to fly as they had done from Fareham? Janey chattered while Helen went over all those miserable calculations. It was almost dark when she went back to the room in which her father sat alone.

"Have you not gone, Helen? I thought I heard the Précepteur asking for you at the door."

"I am not going, papa." She came and sat down by him in the dark, which hid her countenance from him. She laid her hand softly upon his. "Papa, they have come."

"How you startle me, Helen!" he cried querulously. "Oh, I remember: the English visitors. Well! I hope you were discreet and did as I said?"

"You were right," she said, "and I was wrong. I thought it so unlikely; but don't they say here that it is the unlikely things that happen? Papa, one of them is Charley Ashton, whom we met at Sainte-Barbe."

"Good Lord!" he cried, starting from his chair; then after a pause reseated himself. "I will keep out of the way," he said. "I regretted afterwards that I left Sainte-Barbe when I did. Charley Ashton is not the sort of fellow to betray any one: and I think," he said with a half laugh, "that he was very, very much struck with you. I should not wonder if that was why he has come back to this neighbourhood—although Sainte-Barbe is a good way from here."

These words scarcely conveyed any meaning to Helen's ear. All she made out was that her father was not so much alarmed, not so thoroughly roused to think of his own welfare as he ought to be.

"Papa, he got out of the carriage to talk to me. He spoke of you; he said I was to warn you, and that this would be enough: I was to tell you his cousin is with him, Sir John Harvey——"

"My God!" cried Mr. Goulburn. This time he got up, pale as ashes, but fell back, not out of carelessness but weakness. His hands resting upon the table shook it with their trembling. He dropped back again into his chair, his under lip falling, his face like that of a dead man.

"He has been a sufferer, and he is very bitter. If he gets any suspicion he will not

be silenced. This is what Mr. Ashton said.
I don't know what it means, papa," said
Helen with a quiver of her lip, "nor why
any man who comes here, any man! should
make you run away as if you were a criminal——"
"It is because I am a criminal, Helen."
"Papa!"
"No, no," he said, trying to smile, "not
that. God knows I never meant any harm;
but I was led on from one thing to another,
and nobody can understand another man's
temptations. I went farther than I should
have done. Some people—that could not
afford it—were brought into trouble through
me; that is all, Helen. I owe a great deal
of money, as I told you. This Sir John
is one of the people. It is nothing but
money, money. If I had killed their fathers
and mothers they would not have felt it half
so much. It is money, as I tell you—nothing
but money. And now I must get up and
go away from here. Ill, and getting old, and
tired, tired to death——"
He put down his head into his hands,
which trembled; his whole stooping figure
shook. He was certainly thinner, weaker,
and far older in appearance than when they
came to Latour. Helen sat beside him, looking at him with a wretched half-sympathy.
Perhaps, up to this moment, it had been herself she had been thinking of most, herself
who had done no harm, who did not even
know why it was that she was to be driven
from the new roof where she had found refuge. Now her mind turned, but with a
languid misery, to realise what her father was
feeling. He was himself the cause of his own
sufferings. But did that make that easier to
bear?
"Poor papa!" she said, involuntarily
touching with her hand his trembling arm.
Yes, he was ill, and getting old, and how
natural if he were tired, tired to death? All
Helen's present trouble fell into a sort of
dull and aching pity for him, who was the
cause of it. She sat for a little while in dead
silence; and then she said, "What are we
to do?"
It was some time before he made her any
reply; he was panting for breath; there was
a hectic colour on his cheeks like fever. "If
you had but stayed in the house!" he said.
"What did you want with these people at
the Château? They were strangers—and you
should avoid strangers. It will always be
like this wherever we go. You will make
friends, and then you will wonder that it is so
much harder to go away. What right have

we to make friends? we cannot get any good
out of them. We who must be like this,
without any place to rest the sole of our feet,
till we"—he paused a moment—"till I die."
A faint dolorous wonder had crossed the
mind of Helen. She would not leave him,
nothing would make her leave him, lonely as
he was. But that momentary pause, and
the substitution of I for we, touched his
daughter's heart. She put her hand again
softly on his arm.
"Papa, we could not go away by night, all
this long, dreadful way—and Janey. If we
were to go early, early in the morning, would
not that do? It is not so cold now, and the
diligence goes so early. That would be best,
not to attract any attention; or if we could
leave her with Margot till we got settled——"
"Leave—my child!—do you want me to
leave my child?" he cried, as if she had
suggested something cruel—"till we get settled?" and he laughed. "The only use of
that would be to give them a clue to trace
us by. We could not live without news of
her, and letters are destructive. Do you
think we could have been quiet here so long,
so quiet, if there had been letters coming
after us? No, we must go altogether when
we go. But suppose that I were to keep
out of the way," he said in a half entreating
tone, "suppose that I kept my room, suppose—I don't know what is the matter with
me—I have lost my courage. This man cannot stay very long with the Vieux-bois, Helen.
Don't you think if I were to shut myself up,
to see no one? You could say I was ill——"
"He is going to marry Cécile; they will
talk of us, they will describe you, and there
will be Mr. Ashton who knows us. It might
be right—I mean not very wrong, for me—
but he, why should he tell lies for us?" said
Helen mournfully.
Her father recovered himself as by a
miracle. He sat up in his chair, and his nervous trembling ceased. He even laughed.
"I will manage Charley Ashton," he said.
Shortly after he was summoned to see
Antoine, who had come with the notary to
receive the money which had been agreed
upon as the price of his services as Baptiste's
remplaçant. Mr. Goulburn got up quite
revived and restored, and went to his own
room, where the two men awaited him. It
was his bedroom, but also his sitting-room;
the small business he had occupied himself
with, since his arrival in Latour, having been
all performed there. In a large old bureau,
which stood between the window and the
fireplace, were all his papers, his writing-

materials, the few books he had picked up. In a drawer of this bureau he kept his money. Probably there were none of the secondary vexations of his ruined life which affected him so much as the necessity of keeping his money in a drawer, and counting it out to every claimant; but the sums that were necessary for their living were so small that as yet he had not been much disturbed by it. This was the first occasion on which he had taken any serious sum from the stores with which he had provided himself. The notary sat at the table. Antoine, striding across a chair, placed himself in front of the window, between his companion and Mr. Goulburn. He watched every movement of the Englishman, who took no heed of his dark looks. "This is one of the worst of your French customs," he said pettishly. "In England I should have given him a cheque on my bankers without any trouble." It was not in English flesh and blood not to say this, though, even as he said it, Mr. Goulburn remembered with a bitter pang, what so often he managed to forget, that no English banker would honour a cheque of his, or pay any regard save that of hostile curiosity to his dishonoured name.

"Monsieur, it will be long before a peasant will trust to your cheques; it is not always even that they care for bank-notes. Gold, hard gold, that is what they like best; but Antoine has education, and is very well content with the bank-notes."

"Perfectly content," said Antoine. He had his eyes fixed upon the movements of l'Anglais. Mr. Goulburn took out one thing after another from the drawer. First, the morocco letter-case which he had sent Helen to fetch on the night of the flight from Fareham, then a pocket-book bursting with papers; then, finally, the thing he was looking for, his cheque-book, which he took out with a sigh.

"In England I should fill up one of these forms, and all would be done," he said, showing it.

Antoine bent curiously forward to look at it. "Is it money?" he said, with some eagerness, yet suspicion; a book of bank-notes! It seemed not at all unnatural to Antoine that an Englishman should travel with such an article at hand.

"Not till Monsieur puts his signature," said the smiling notary. "Look, it is a *livre à souches.* Here is the counterfoil on which Monsieur marks the cipher. It is very ingenious; but in the country in France there is nothing we trust in like *des bons gros sous.*

We like to hear the money tinkle, *n'est-ce pas,* Antoine? Not that I say anything against a bank-note, and an English bank-note, Monsieur; that is well known to be unimpeachable all over the world."

"Do not be afraid," said Mr. Goulburn, putting back the cheque-book and the morocco case, and opening the pocket-book— "these are notes of the Bank of France." Antoine looked at it, devouring it from under his heavy eyebrows. What countless sums might there not be in that drawer! First, the leather case, no doubt full of *valeurs* of one kind or another; then the book of English money, half as thick as a *paroissien;* then the bursting pocket-book full of French notes. There is no end to the wealth of those other English; and to think that all that should lie almost within reach of a man's hand, in a drawer against Père Goudron's outer wall!

Mr. Goulburn took out the notes one by one, three notes for five hundred francs each —a fortune! but nothing to the riches that remained. He took them out from a sheaf of others carelessly, closing the pocket-book again and laying it down quite at his ease, not at all excited by the possession of so much money, almost within reach of the dangerous eyes that were watching him.

"Here is your money, my *bon homme,*" he said. "M. le Notaire tells me all the formalities have been gone through. Do not put it away in a drawer, as I have to do, but invest it, Antoine, invest it; put it somewhere where it will bring you in good interest. That is what we call a very pretty little nest egg in England. If you manage it well, if you take care of it, there is no telling to what it may grow."

"Monsieur gives you very excellent advice," said the notary. "I hope you will take it, Antoine. There are a few little things against you, as indeed there are against most young men, but I hope you will clear them all off, and come back to the village when your service is done with your *livret* in the best possible order. You have helped to give peace and comfort to one house, and that should be a pleasant thing to think of."

Antoine received all these good wishes and good counsels with an air of pre-occupation. Fifteen hundred francs, it was a fortune! still, what it was was nothing to what was in the pocket-book which lay so carelessly on the bureau. A thirst, a hunger got into his mind. Was it his fault? was it not rather that of the Englishman with his careless ways? Never, never, in all his life, had he seen what he believed to be so much money before.

Instinctively his eyes glanced round under cover of his dark brows. There was the window on one side, a window which gave upon the street, within reach of a man of Antoine's height; and on the other the door. The bed was at the other side of the room. A clever person might get through a great deal of work without even awaking the sleeper, without doing any more harm.

Helen went out to the door an hour or two later, when her father—who complained of fatigue and agitation, and was querulous and peevish with her, as if the visit of the English strangers was her fault—had gone to bed. It was still not very late. Everything was in full activity at the Lion d'Or, and the sound of the voices, and now and then a scrap of song, still sounded into the quiet air of the night, softened by the distance and by the milder atmosphere, humid and soft, which had succeeded the long frosts. It made the girl's heart beat to see some one standing waiting for her in the shadow of the house. The moon was shining behind, and all in front of Père Goudron's was in the blackest shadow. Helen had never had a lover. It was not of that she thought now, as she opened the door cautiously; but yet there was something in this meeting which made her heart beat strangely. Young Ashton came close to the door.

"I have told them I always walk at night; they think everything possible to the eccentricity of an Englishman," he said with a half smile, "so that I am at your disposal whatever you may be going to do."

"We are to do nothing," she said. "He will keep his room; he will say he is ill. Indeed, he is not well, Mr. Ashton, something is the matter with him, I cannot tell what. He is nervous, he is not himself; he says he has no courage to go away. Perhaps you will not stay long at the Château?"

"You wish us to be gone?" he said, with a tone of vexation.

"Can I help it?" said Helen. "Do you think I shall have a moment's rest till you are gone?—or after?" she added mournfully; "for how can I tell who may come next?—some one not so kind as you."

"That is what I think," he said anxiously, "you will never feel safe. If it were I that was the danger, whatever it might cost me, I would go; but it is not I. It is John, and he has come to see his future wife. One cannot expect him to go, do you think? I am not in his case."

He said this with such marked meaning, and looked at Helen so closely, that she could

not but remark it, and wonder, with a nervous tremor, what did he mean?

"Miss Goulburn," he said, "this is not the time to talk of such things, is it? I am going back to India soon; and I want to marry. I know it sounds brutal what I am saying. If you will marry me, it would be one way of settling all this. We could see him placed comfortably somewhere out of the way, in Spain perhaps, and you would not need to go home to be troubled by what is said. It is wicked that you should be dragged about, you so innocent as you are, flying from one place to another. I cannot bear to think of it. Even your name—— Will you take mine, Helen? If you would do it, I cannot tell you how happy it would make me. I never had any hope; but this has always been in my mind since that school feast when you were only a little girl."

Helen did not remember anything about the school feast. She was perplexed by this reference to it which clouded over the sharp distinctness of the proposal which preceded it. And when she paused she could not speak; she was struck dumb, half by the sudden business-like character of the proposal, and half by the wonder of it. She had never thought (had she? she was not so sure after the first moment) of anything of the sort. She stood bewildered, and gazed blankly at him in the blackness of the night.

"I have been too hasty, and frightened you. I knew I should; but how can I help it? there is no time to lose. Tell me only one thing: you are not going to marry any one else?"

"Oh, no, no," said Helen; then she added simply, "No one has ever asked me before."

He came a little closer and took her hand. "I thought you must have seen at Sainte-Barbe," he said. "I was half out of my mind with joy to see you, and next day miserable when I found you had gone. Helen, if you think you could like me, there will be plenty, plenty of love on my side. And think what a motive I should have to take care of your father. We could settle him somewhere—you and I together—where he would be safe, quite safe. And after a while they will give up thinking about him. It would be for his advantage," said the young man earnestly. "Give me a little hope, and I will keep John off—he shall never suspect. No," cried Charley vehemently, "I will not make any condition. I will keep John off, anyhow; you may calculate upon me. I will be your watchman to keep danger away, whether you give me hope or not."

"Mr. Ashton," said Helen, "you are very, very kind. How can I give you what I have not got? Hope! I have not any. Before you came I felt as if I must give up, and let things happen as they would."

"But you don't feel that now?" he said eagerly; "you think it is worth while to try again, to fight your best, however hard it may be, not to give in? That is what you feel now?"

"Yes; it is you that have given me hope; not I that can give it you."

"Don't you see it is the same thing?" he cried. "It is because we are two of us—not one poor individual standing alone, but two to do everything together: that makes all the difference in the world."

Helen did not speak, but she felt it, she could not tell why. Yes, there was a difference. The burden was lighter; there was a change in the air; the road did not seem to lead away entirely into the darkness as it had done an hour before. Two of them!— was that the reason of the change?

"Helen! that would be all, almost all, I wanted—if you feel so too."

She did not make any direct reply; but she said, "I could not go to India, and leave him. It would not be possible to leave him. If he were well, if he were safe—but how could I leave him now?"

"He would wish it," said young Ashton very decidedly, "if he knew. He is not a bad man, Helen." (He paused here, and made a little mental reservation with natural severity.) "He does not want to make you wretched, dragging you after him. He would wish it if he knew."

There was another pause, and then Helen abandoned this subject altogether, and said, with a little quiver in her voice which—was it possible?—sounded half like laughter, "You were—perhaps they thought it possible—to have been the *future* of Thérèse?"

"Folly!" he cried. "John thought it would answer; as if any Englishman would make such a bargain: the woods to look after, and a very pretty young lady! What would he have said, I wonder, if he had been brought in cold blood to Cécile? But he did not know my heart was full of some one else; that is his only excuse."

At this moment a bell tinkled inside, and Helen started; he was standing very near to her now, close up in the shadow of the doorway, two that looked like one. And she did not make any objection. But now she disengaged herself softly. "It is papa who wants me," she said.

"Then it is a bargain, dear. I will be on the watch; I will keep off John. I will come and see what you think to-morrow night."

"Good night," she whispered. It sounded like an echo of the last word he had said.

Mr. Goulburn had raised himself half out of his bed, his eyes were feverish and shining. "Who was that?" he said. "You were talking to some one at the door."

Helen stood with a candle in her hand, which threw a vivid light upon her face, bringing out its soft brilliancy of tint, the blush that hung over it like a faint rose-shadow, the dewy dazzlement of agitation in the eyes amid the surrounding darkness. She said very softly, with a little catch of her breath, "It was Mr. Ashton, papa."

Mr. Goulburn lay back upon his pillows with a relieved face; he laughed. "That is all right," he said—"now I shall sleep in peace. I have two guardians instead of one."

"Papa thinks so *too*," Helen said to herself, as she went into the room where Janey was sleeping. It had all been very sudden, and she did not understand it; but there was a wonderful difference. "It is because there are two of us—not one standing alone." Were there ever words that meant so much? And papa thought so *too*.

<h3 style="text-align:center">CHAPTER XIV.</h3>

"HARFORD? No, I don't know anybody of the name," Sir John had said; but while Charley was out after dinner, exercising that inalienable privilege of an Englishman to do absurd things, which everybody recognises in France, he heard a great deal about the English family in the village which made him think. Helen was said to have spoken of Fareham, which Sir John knew very well; and Ashton had recognised this mysterious English girl, whose presence here was so unaccountable. And there was a father in bad health—and a child. What could such people want at Latour? "You shall see her at dinner," Cécile said; but she did not come to dinner, and Sir John, who had frowned at the prospect of a dinner-party, as he chose to call it, on the first night of his arrival, frowned still more when Helen's apologies were made, with great earnestness and regrets far more eloquent than anything Helen would have thought of expressing, by the wife of the Précepteur. If she was to come, why didn't she come? What was the meaning of it? Could it be some entanglement of Charley's, his cousin thought.

"Had they anything to do with Fareham?" he asked late that night, when

Charley had come in, glowing and radiant, from his night walk. " I don't understand about these English people in the village. Where did you meet them? who are they? I don't want any equivocal people here, in Cécile's very village. What could they have to do with Fareham? I never heard the name there."

" I met them somewhere in the parish," said Charley evasively. " I forget exactly in which house. You don't know all the people in Fareham parish. I believe it was at a school feast——"

Of how much service that school feast had been! Sir John was more satisfied, but uncertain still.

" The father is ill," he said.

" So the Comtesse said," said Charley with caution. He was too much on his guard to commit himself.

" A strange place for a sick man, not a doctor, except the parish doctor, within thirty miles. What in the name of wonder could have brought them to Latour?"

" I suppose," said Charley, " it is a very cheap place."

" Cheap? there is something in that," said Sir John. Then he paused, and, fixing his eyes upon his cousin, " I tell you what," he said, " I shouldn't wonder a bit if it was another victim of that scoundrel Goulburn, some poor wretch who has lost every penny, who has dragged himself here, to die perhaps. Don't you think it would be civil to go and see him, as he is ill? They take no end of interest in him here."

" There is no hurry about it," said Charley in dismay; but Sir John was very persistent. He spoke of it again next morning, and the proposal was received with enthusiasm by the ladies.

" We will go together," Cécile said, who indeed could not contain her impatience till her friend had seen and given an opinion upon her lover. Sir John was a fine, big, imposing Englishman, a pattern of all that a Sir John ought to be—somewhat easily put out in temper, and therefore affording all the excitement of dramatic uncertainty to the vivacious Frenchwoman, who had never as yet found the uncertainty more than piquant. She liked him the better that he was not always on the watch to pay her little attentions like the men she was accustomed to, and prized his approbation all the more that it was so doubtful, and that it took so much trouble to secure it. Cécile was very anxious to exhibit her large, important lover to Helen; and she was also eager to secure Helen's

admiration and approval, of which she felt no doubt. That he was not as the other frivolous young *fiancés*, or even as this cousin, Cécile felt proudly confident. Sir John, it may be added, was a man of thirty-five, *rangé*, serious, a public man, a personage. In all these points of view Cécile's young bosom swelled with pride in him. As has been already insisted upon, virtue, seriousness, and duty are, amongst at least one important portion of the upper classes, of the very highest fashion in France.

Charley did all he could to change their purpose. He said, with a little hesitation, that he had seen Miss Harford, that he had stopped to ask for her father during his walk, and that the invalid meant to keep his bed for a day or two. This, however, had no effect upon the party, which set out very cheerfully in the noonday sunshine, after the second breakfast, to show the village, and to see the English friends who had become so important in the life of Cécile and Thérèse. We have not space now to tell with what swift and silent observation the Comtesse and her daughters had scrutinised and decided upon Charley. At the first glance he had succeeded in " pleasing " Thérèse, who knew very well that it was her mother's purpose to marry her, according to the simple formula of her nation, and who at first believed M. Charles to have come to the château with the same ideas. In this point of view all the ladies found him quite *convenable*, but —— The Comtesse herself questioned Sir John very closely when his cousin went out after dinner for that walk which quite chimed in with her ideas of the English character.

" M. Charles is aware of the situation, of course?" Madame la Comtesse said. " It is well that there should not be any mistake on this point. He knows my intention in respect to Thérèse, and the dispositions of the will, &c. So far as appearances go, I find him very suitable, and that he will be pleasing to Thérèse is probable. There is nothing against the arrangement. But we must know how it appears to him on his side. There must be no step taken by us which does not meet a response. M. Charles on his part has he expressed his sentiments? Does he find my daughter pleasing to him on his side? It is necessary to be more explicit on the part of the gentleman: has he given you to understand——"

" Oh dear no!" cried Sir John, alarmed. He had sounded Charley, but had not got a promising response, and now thought it wisest to ignore the plan altogether. "Oh, certainly not. I have not said a word to him, my dear Comtesse. Fancy bringing an Englishman here with the idea that he was on sight! Oh dear no! I brought him on the chance that they might fancy each other, the most likely thing in the world—a pretty girl like Thérèse, and a nice young fellow. It was the most natural thing that they should fall in love with each other."

"Ah, fall in loofe, that was not my idea," said Madame de Vieux-bois—Sir John spoke his native language, in which she was not an expert. And after this conversation the Comtesse put her daughters on their guard. "Mes enfans," she said privately, "we will postpone the question. Ce Monsieur Charles ne me plaît pas. There is something about him—— And I find, besides, that it is too soon to think of marrying Thérèse; she is but seventeen. It will be enough to lose thee, ma Cécile—enough for one year."

Madame la Comtesse was far too careful a mother to permit her child's thoughts to dwell upon any one who might be found unresponsive. The girls understood more or less, and they declared their mamma to have reason, as indeed she had in the fullest sense of the word. This, however, subdued Thérèse a little; not that she felt disappointed in respect to Charley Ashton, but that she no longer felt herself in the important position of being about to make the great decision of her life. She could not take Helen aside, as she had intended to do, with pretty airs of gravity, and ask her advice with solemn meaning. "Est-ce qu'il te plaît?" she had intended to say, curving her young brows with all the seriousness that became so momentous a question. She felt that she was coming down from an anticipated elevation, when she had no such important decision to make. And Cécile, too, was disappointed. The crisis was *manqué*. It failed in the double seriousness, the weighty character she had intended it to have. If they were but a little more reasonable, these Englishmen—a little more amenable to rule! All the time, however, Cécile piqued herself very much upon the delightful fact that her John and she had come together by no arrangement, but had for their part proceeded on strictly English principles, and fallen in lofe.

It would be difficult to describe the embarrassment of Helen, receiving this party of visitors, meeting the friendly enthusiasm of her young companions with the knowledge of her own secret, which she could not disclose to them, in her heart, and with the very

much more dreadful secret of which she was the guardian, pressing itself upon her, confusing her mind and weighing heavily upon all her thoughts. She dared not look at Charley at all. To have met him even alone after the revelations of last night, after the strange incomprehensible change in their position towards each other which it had brought about, would have been confusing beyond measure. But when added to all this there was the terrible figure of Sir John inspecting her with British suspicion, asking her in every look, Who are you? what business have you here? and the consciousness of her father lurking in his room, whom the mistaking of a door, a wrong turning, might betray, it may be supposed that no inexperienced girl, standing upon the threshold of her life among things unrealised, could have had a more terrible half hour than had Helen, alone with this group, having to parry all their questions and meet all their looks without breaking down utterly or running away. She had thought it best to send Janey out to the garden, lest the child, who would have been of so much assistance to her, might make some unwitting disclosure. And there she stood alone, clasping her little delicate hands together, to meet them all, to conceal what was in her—alas! to deceive them. The tears were trembling very near poor Helen's eyes, her voice wavered now and then as if it would break altogether, her little figure swayed; but yet she stood firm, though she could not tell how she did it. The girls put down her trouble naturally to her father's illness. They kissed her and whispered sympathy into her ears. "Du courage!" they said, with tears of tender pity and fellow-feeling. "If mamma could but come herself!" But they had no doubt that mamma could send something that would be of use. "It is the emotion of yesterday," they concluded, with all the ease of spectators. And then Sir John had to be told the incident of yesterday and the goodness of Monsieur. This was a blessed relief to Helen, whom he had begun to interrogate about Fareham and all she knew about it. "I suppose you did not know the last people that lived there? One of those great *nouveaux riches*, those men that live like princes on other people's money. He turned out to be a swindl——"

"Helen," whispered Cécile, drawing her apart before the sentence was completed, "Est-ce qu'il te plaît? I want you to give me your most honest opinion. Je veux qu'il te plaît! Tell me exactly, exactly what you think—for you must like him," said Sir John's bride, with a pretty flush of impetuous eagerness. Thérèse, who had believed that she too would have had the same question to put, had surprised certain turns of the head—certain looks which Charley addressed to her friend—and she was curious beyond measure, and bursting with a thousand questions. When the visit was over poor Helen saw them go away, waving her hand to them from the door, keeping up her smile to the last moment. She did not lose the last suspicious glance of Sir John, who looked (accidentally) at her father's window with all the force of an inquiry, but she scarcely got the comfort of Ashton's anxious, tender look of sympathy which told all his story to Thérèse. She was at the end of her strength, but nevertheless, she had to rouse herself to go to her father, who wanted to know every particular of the interview.

"I heard Harvey's voice," Mr. Goulburn said. "There was always something objectionable in his voice. Big Philistine! Cécile de Vieux-bois is a great deal too good for him. He has dined with me dozens of times, but I think it was always in town, and at my club. He could not have any suspicions. Did he seem to you to have any suspicion, Helen?"

"He had a great deal of suspicion, papa, but I don't think he knew what he suspected. He can't understand what we are doing here. Provided," said Helen, with a little French idiom of which she was unconscious, "provided he does not come another time and take us unawares."

"He shall not take me unawares, you may trust to me, Helen; I shall not budge till the big brute is gone."

Her father spoke in a reassuring tone, as if promising for her sake to abjure all imprudence. Their positions seemed to have changed, she could not tell how. She was no longer the wistful follower in a flight, the motive of which she was ignorant of. One would have thought rather that it was some indiscretion of hers that had brought this danger upon him, some rashness which he was too generous to reproach her with. I will do my best for you, you may trust to me, was what he seemed to be saying; and this brought the confusion in her mind to a climax. She went about all the long day after like one in a dream.

"It cannot be for cheapness these people have come here," said Sir John to Charley. "You heard that story about the substitute? That does not look like poverty. Besides, I don't believe the man is ill. The girl didn't look as if it were true. He is keeping out of our way. Depend upon it there is something shady about him. I think I've seen the girl before."

"Very likely; she is very young, but she has been out a little," said Charley hurriedly, anxious to avoid any following out of the subject. "One meets everybody one time or another. Even I, who have spent my time in anything but balls——"

"Yes; by the way, how is it you seem to know the girl so well?" said Sir John.

"I wish, if it's all the same to you," cried Charley, out of patience, "that you'd speak a little more civilly. I don't see why you should call a young lady whom you know nothing of, 'the girl,' in that contemptuous way. Yes; it does matter to me. I don't know that I ever met any one in my life that I admired so much."

"Whew!" Sir John gave a prolonged whistle of amazement; "why, she's not fit to hold the candle to Thérèse," he said; then added drily, "the more reason why I should find out all about them. I am a great deal older than you are, and I don't mean you to make a fool of yourself if I can help it, Charley."

"I think you had better mind your own business," the other said, in high revolt.

And thus Sir John acquired a double motive. He questioned Cécile at great length, and even took her to task for giving her confidence so easily. "If it should turn out, as is most likely to be the case, a person entirely unworthy of your friendship!" he said. The Château was all in agitation over this subject. The girls indignantly protesting, the mother disposed to take alarm. Decidedly the possession of a serious, rangé, important English lover of thirty-five brings its penalties with it; but perhaps, indeed, a lover of any age, however free and easy in his own relationships, would have been equally anxious to guard the lady endowed with his valuable affections from any connection with inappropriate acquaintances. For the moment, however, his zeal did not increase the comfort of the house.

The day was feverish and long—how long and feverish and full of alarm and apprehension perhaps only Helen knew. She sat at watch at her window all the day, trembling whenever she saw any one approach from the direction of the Château. In the afternoon Charley came in and consoled her, but rather with a repetition of that sentiment about two being better than one, than with any more immediately satisfactory information. Helen thought the day would never come to an end; and there seemed no comfort even in the fact that sooner or later it must come to an end, for what was there to hope but that to-morrow would be like it? After dinner, when the village was all still, her father looked cautiously into the sitting-room. "I must get a breath of air," he said, half apologetically, half reproachfully. It was as if this imprisonment to his room was Helen's fault.

"Papa, I don't think I can bear it another day. Let us go away, let us go away!" she cried.

"I thought it was you who objected to going away," he said peevishly.

Helen sat down again before her little lamp at the table. This time she had some darning to do. She sat and listened for every step, for every breath. Oh, to go away, to go away! she said to herself. To go where? She could not tell. Was there safety anywhere? Was there any spot on earth where this sickening, shameful danger, this concealment would not come again? Was it not out of the world, away from life and its torments altogether, where alone they could be safe? After a while Mr. Goulburn came back. He was nervous too, and shaken by the alarm that seemed in the air.

"I don't seem happy in the village to-night," he said, "though it is all as quiet as usual. I think that big bully must use up all the air for his own breathing, I can't get any." He opened the *persiennes* as he spoke, then drew them close again. "I think I shall go into the garden, Helen. I must get breath somewhere. I have shut the front door. Go to bed. I shall go and sit in the summer-house to get my breath."

"Will you take some of the Comtesse's drops, papa. She said they were so good."

"Ether," he said; "simple ether; it smells too strong. What do I want with your old wife's medicines? No, I'll go and sit out in the garden and get my breath. Poor child, you are tired, and it is no wonder. But all is safe now for the night, Helen; go to bed."

All was safe for the night. The dreadful day was over with all its terrors—everything was still. The village had gone to sleep all the earlier that it had been so late on the night before. Helen felt too much alarmed to open the door again to look out for Charley Ashton. She took her father's advice passively, and went to her room, where Janey was sleeping peacefully. Something, she could not tell what, kept her from undressing. She lay down upon her bed to

wait till her father should come in from the garden. He might want something before he went finally to rest. But Helen was worn out with the long trial of the day, and lying across her bed fully dressed, she dropped to sleep.

All was safe for the night—so some one else thought who was standing under the shadow of Père Goudron's wall. The moon was veiled and dim, but yet was shining and casting a shadow more dark than the ordinary darkness of the night. It was not possible to see what it was at the corner under the window, but something moved; it was as if a part of the darkness detached itself slowly from the rest; where all was black, a something blacker than the air, yet separate from the wall, rising upward. It moved noiselessly across the front of the house. All was quiet, so still that a breath might have been heard, but nothing was audible. A faint glimmer showed where Mr. Goulburn in his impatience had opened the *persiennes*. He had drawn them close again, but he had not fastened them. He had a contempt for bolts and bars in this quiet place. They were open, and the window was open, showing a little glimmer of light. But in the darkness even that far-away glimmer showed. The moving thing below put up a hand and cautiously, softly opened the unfastened *persiennes*, then climbed up noiselessly, a long, dark, undistinguishable figure, into the room, drawing the shutters close behind. Was all safe? There was a pause, and the empty room became full of a living presence, a breath, a danger. Beyond the folding-doors, which were closed, Helen slept profoundly the sleep of utter weariness. Across the passage the faint little ray of the *veilleuse* shone steadily through the half-opened door. The question was—did any one lie there, sleeping or waking? The intruder took what was, in the circumstances, a long time to consider. Then he advanced silently. To himself it seemed that the whole house crouched and shivered under his feet, but Helen, fast asleep, heard nothing; and if out in the garden a vague sound reached her father's ears, he imagined it was only Helen moving about her bedroom, where her light was still burning. That watching light seemed to make all safe, and the little *veilleuse*, on the other hand, guarded the empty chamber. The thief trembled before it. He paused and wiped his forehead, not daring to confront it. But he had gone too far now not to go on. The man's heart, which was beating wildly with excitement, gave a great

5

jump when, peeping in, he saw the room vacant, the bed unoccupied. He went in and closed the door.

All were sleeping quietly in the house, except Père Goudron, who lay quiet enough, but not asleep, thinking of the folly of l'Anglais, who had given away so much money for the sake of a young man who was nothing to him, and wondering in what way he could manage to secure some of those same superabundant riches for himself. He could not himself violently have robbed l'Anglais or any one else. But he, too, had seen the book with the French notes, and he longed for a share of them. He was turning over in his mind what fable he could invent, what tale of poverty he could tell to beguile some more of those notes out of the rich man's pocket. He heard the creak, the startling sound of movement, but thought nothing of it. His lodgers did not keep the regular hours he did; they were like all the English, early one night, late another, never to be relied upon. But he lay still and pondered, intent upon inventing some story by which he, too, might get a share of the spoil.

Mr. Goulburn, for his part, sat on the bench in the garden, and tried, as he had said, to get his breath. It had never been so bad before. His heart laboured, thumping like a steam-engine, creaking and struggling as if the machinery was all rusty and out of gear. What was the meaning of it? There had never been anything the matter with his heart till that old witch at the Château decided that he had heart disease. She was not an old witch; but that is how men of middle age describe their female contemporaries who have displeased them. The moon was high in the sky, but veiled and watery, giving a sort of milky whiteness to the atmosphere rather than light. Under this faint pale glimmer he sat with a small acacia waving its long leaflets over him. It must be a sultry night—certainly there was no air to breathe; he could not get any. Harvey with his big British lungs must have exhausted it, he thought, with a faint joke in his mind in the midst of his bodily distress. No air to breathe. He bethought himself by-and-by of the Comtesse's drops, which, after all, might do some good. At first he thought he would call Helen to get them for him. Then a pitying recollection of her wan face crossed his mind. He would not disturb her, poor child; he would go himself. He rose and came in slowly, his labouring heart sounding in the stillness, his very limbs feeble with its excited action.

A moment more and the quiet of the sleeping house, was broken by a hideous commotion. There was a sound of a door pushed open, a loud exclamation, a momentary conflict of voices, the door dashed back against the wall. Then a wild, long cry, a dull thud upon the floor. By that time Père Goudron had got out of his bed, and was calling upon Blanchette and Ursule, and scrambling for a light, and Helen, waking in wild terror out of her sleep, had sprung up and seized her candle. She was so transported with anxiety and terror that the voices that followed conveyed no information to her ear; but M. Goudron heard the *persiennes* dashed open, and a muffled leap into the street. Next moment Helen's cries resounded through the house and rang out into the night.

"Papa, papa, speak to me!" she cried; "speak to me, papa!"

Madame Dupré, who had just fastened up her last shutter, heard it, and rushed to the door—then ran back again and dragged Baptiste out of bed in his first sleep.

"L'Anglais!—something has happened to l'Anglais," she said.

And then by degrees one house after another woke, and eager heads peered forth at the doors and windows. Baptiste, rushing across the road half-dressed, with Auguste at his heels, was called to from one side and another in a dozen startled voices.

"What is it? What has happened?" they all asked, breathless. He answered only by repeating what his mother had told him.

"L'Anglais—something has happened to l'Anglais," Baptiste said.

Two men were coming down the road from the Château. It was not much more than ten o'clock, and Sir John had come out with Charley, much against the will of the latter, to smoke his cigar.

"I'll take a turn with you," the Baronet had said. "It's muggy to-night, with all those trees about. If you had hit it off with Thérèse, Charley, I'd have advised you to thin these woods. But it's no use thinking about that. What an odd piece of luck, however, that you should have found this Miss—Miss——"

"Helen," said Ashton, with a bitterness he could scarcely restrain. Rather this familiarity than to speak of her by a false name.

"Miss—Helen—that's it. Cécile never says the other name. You don't say you know the father, Charley? I'd advise you to find out what sort of person he is, and all about him, before you go any farther, old man. It is queer that just at the other one's door, so to speak, you should have found this Miss —Helen."

" I wish you would not speak of the other one, John. It is very disrespectful to a very charming young lady. There has never been any other one. You offend me when you talk so, by offending her. I have the greatest reverence for the ladies here— both——"

" You need not be so particular. She would not be offended. She knows very well that this marriage is *manqué*, and she is not inconsolable. But, look here: you must not go a step further till you know all particulars. I say, what is that? What an infernal row!" said Sir John.

The sound of the sudden cry affronting the silence, and even the fall that followed, ringing out into the great quiet with all the intensity of a sudden calamity, reached them both, though they were scarcely within sight of Père Goudron's house. They rushed on without another word, Charley quickening his steps to a run, as they perceived where the tumult was. By this time dark figures were coming out into the street from the cottages near, and everything was in commotion. M. Goudron's door stood wide open; the *persiennes* had been thrown open also, and what seemed a flood of light poured out into the street. Charley rushed in, and Sir John followed. In the midst of a group of eager spectators a pale figure was lying on the bed. He had struck his forehead against something as he fell, and a drop or two of blood slowly congealing upon it showed the blow. His lips were open, hanging apart, dry and parched, his eyes half closed, and showing a dull, inexpressive light. The two Englishmen went forward, joining themselves to the group. The village doctor, half dressed, stood holding a mirror to the dry lips. Old Goudron, like a living skeleton, with a nervous quiver in his old bones, held a candle, like Time or Death himself assisting at the death-bed. In one corner Ursule was praying on her knees. Helen stood, pallid as the dead face itself, supporting the pillows on which he was propped, at the head of the bed.

Sir John was slow to take in the chief feature of the scene; he mastered everything else before he perceived that : the doctor, with the little mirror in his hand, upon which no stain of living breath was to be seen; the old bony figure by the bed ; the young daughter, silent and distraught ; then his eyes fixed themselves on the face of the man round whom they had all collected.

His sudden shout shook the room. He cried out in astonishment, in consternation and horror. "My God! it is Goulburn himself!" Sir John said.

<h2>CHAPTER XV.</h2>

MR. GOULBURN was dead. It was hard to tell how it had happened. There was the mark on his forehead of a blow, but to all appearance it was a blow accidentally inflicted as he fell, and not done by any hand, and it was not sufficient to have been the cause of his death. That the state of his heart sufficiently explained. But whether it was the sight of the thief which had brought on the final paroxysm, or whether they had come into actual conflict, or if the disease was so far advanced that any trifling shock would have done it, it was more difficult to decide. All the drawers of the bureau were found pulled out, and the one in which the money had been kept was rifled. Even on this point, however, the juge de paix found it difficult to refrain from blaming the deceased for his own loss. The keys had been left in the drawer—could anything be more foolish? it was a premium upon robbery; the shutters unfastened, so that any one could push them apart ; the window open within that, the room left vacant, protected only by the *veilleuse*, and the things in the drawers. It was the Englishman himself who had laid a trap for the robber, who had invited him, actually invited him to come and help himself; but he had fallen into the trap which he had laid. It was difficult for the prudent Frenchman not to breathe a fervent "served him right," with such variety of expression as the exigencies of more elaborate language required ; but no trace could be found of the thief and possible murderer. He had evidently jumped from the window, leaving the shutters open and the room fully displayed, but it was not till after this that the village had been roused. Père Goudron had heard the leap but nothing more. In the investigation that followed suspicion was directed against Antoine, who had been seen by several persons watching M. Goudron's house ; but it was conclusively proved that Antoine had left that afternoon for the *chef-lieu*, where he had gone to complete all the necessary arrangements for his acceptance as Baptiste's substitute. He had been escorted a league on his way by several of his friends, so on that point there could be no mistake.

The affair of l'Anglais made, as may be supposed, an enormous sensation at Latour.

Nothing like it, so far as was known, had ever happened in the village. The juge de paix sat, *en permanence*, for a number of days examining everybody. They even examined the other Englishmen who were living at the Château, and who declared themselves acquainted with the victim. They were very sharply questioned indeed, so that it occurred to Sir John that they were themselves suspected of the deed, an idea which was the cause of endless discourses on his part, and disquisitions upon the differences between English and French law, very much, it need not be said, to the disadvantage of the latter. The Comtesse for her part scoffed at the *instruction* altogether. She would hear nothing of a possible murder. The man, she said, had death in his face; had she not said so, the first moment she saw him? She had seen him but once, but she had been fully aware what was to be expected; so fully that she had not even urged him to return home, which she would have done had the case seemed to her less serious; for it was better that he should die in Latour than that he should die in the railway, or in an inn, where his daughters would have no one near them but absolute strangers. Madame de Vieux-bois justified her own previsions on this point by sending at once for Helen and little Janey, who, after their father had been laid in the little burying-ground among all the little crosses, with their blue and yellow decorations, came to the Château grateful, but half stupefied with all that had happened to them. Helen, at least, was in this condition, for poor little Janey's despair had been brief, as was natural at her age. But the elder sister had gone through a great many terrible experiences during those two or three days. She had been examined at great length by the magistrate, not only on the circumstances of the fatal night, but on all the antecedents of her family, the reason of her father's residence at Latour, why he had left England, everything about him; and then she had undergone an examination by Sir John, less solemn perhaps, but not less harassing. Sir John was strongly opposed to the engagement which Charley Ashton instantly proclaimed. He declared it to be entirely out of the question, and risked a quarrel not only with his cousin, but with his betrothed and her family. Madame de Vieux-bois, indeed, did not hesitate to agree with him that if the match was so extremely unsuitable as he said, it would be well that it should be put a stop to; but she had herself no responsibility in the matter, and her interest, she confessed, was much

more strong in Helen than in M. Charles, who, she was glad to think, *ne la plaisait pas* from his first appearance. But Cécile and also Thérèse were very eager for Helen's happiness, and very indignant that any attempt should be made against it.

"What!" cried Cécile, beautiful in her generous wrath and wonder, "*les Anglais !*" who believe in nothing but lofe, who blame so much all our arrangements between parents, our ideas upon marriage! You who say there is nothing but a *great passion* which should bring two people together! Look at the book of M. Taine of the Academy, he who is such an admirable writer, who has so much observed England. That is what he says, and I believe it, I! Lofe, that is the true bond, not a similarity of circumstances, the *dot* and the position, and how it will advance one's career. But you—you—an Englishman, so English! you," she cried, with a ring of disappointment in her voice, "you, mon D'John, mon fiancé à moi! that you should try to separate them because my Helen, my poor friend, is— —"

"Come, Cécile," cried Sir John, "is—— that's just it. It's not that she is poor. To be poor is bad enough, I don't say that I approve of it; but it is the bad connection, that is what I dislike. A bankrupt, a—a—swin—— Well, I won't call the dead man names. That is what I object to. I don't say a word against the girl; but, after all, Charley is my cousin and a young fellow with all his life before him, and, hang it all, it is my duty to take care of him."

"And Helen is my friend!" said Cécile. She was shaken in her idea of her lover's perfection, and she was shaken in her confidence in the English nation, and the preeminence of "lofe" in all their affairs—which she had hitherto devoutly believed in, and of which Charley Ashton's conduct had given her delightful assurance. As for Thérèse, she was fully of Cécile's opinion, but yet could not help feeling that if M. Charles had behaved like a reasonable creature, and fulfilled the expectations formed of him before his arrival, it would have been better for himself. For herself Thérèse was glad things had happened so; she was relieved that her mamma had given up all intention of marrying her for that year. But so far as M. Charles was concerned, for him it would have been a great deal better. With this reservation, which on the whole quickened her zeal by mingling it with a grain of pity, Thérèse threw herself generously and warmly into Helen's cause.

When the *instruction* was terminated, and all had been investigated that could be investigated, there was a complete failure in every attempt to trace the criminal. The French law, so suspicious and peremptory, failed just as English criminal proceedings, so much more halting and imperfect, so often fail. Antoine's *alibi* seemed complete. There was no evidence to be found which connected him with the incidents of the fatal night. Mr. Goulburn's English cheque-book was found indeed, torn up and defaced, on the road by which he must have travelled to the *chef-lieu* of the department, but the culprit, whoever he had been, would most likely have travelled by the same road. The only other thing which that culprit had dropped was the morocco letter-case which Helen had brought from her father's room at Fareham on the night of their flight. After all the examinations were over this was restored to her. She came in, carrying it in her hand, to the library where Sir John was spending his morning. It was nearly three weeks after her father's death, and hostile though Sir John was, both to the dead father and the living daughter, it was partly on their account that his visit had been prolonged. He did not choose to leave them in possession of the field, and he was anxious to save Charley, as he said to himself, from the clutches of the girl, who, being Goulburn's daughter, was no doubt an adventuress too. A violent controversy on this subject had, indeed, been going on between the two men when Helen softly opened the door and went in upon them. Sir John was seated at a writing-table with a flushed and angry countenance, while Charley, not less excited, paced about the library. It was a large, long room on the upper floor, with a row of long windows looking out upon the woods and the park. The two men, whose angry voices she had heard without paying much attention to them as she approached, suddenly stopped with embarrassed faces as she made her appearance at the door. Sir John, with an air half of anger, half of surprise, pushed back his chair from the table and looked at her, while Charley hurried to her side and took her hand to lead her forward.

"Did you want me, Helen?" he said, in a tone doubly tender, drawing her hand within his arm. At this little exhibition Sir John uttered an angry "humph!"

"I came to bring you this," said Helen. "I do not know what it is best to do with it. We brought it out of Fareham with us. Papa always said it was Janey's fortune. But if it

is true, as you say, that he owes people money —yes, I know it is true; he told me so himself—this ought, perhaps, to be taken to pay some of them. As for Janey, she is very little, she does not want much now, and I have a hundred a year—that will be enough for her and me."

"Let me see it," said Sir John with some eagerness.

Nobody had been allowed to see the papers so long as they remained in the magistrate's hands. He opened them out with a great deal of interest, shaking one after another out of the case. As he looked at them, opening each in succession, gleams of excitement passed over his face. He made hurried calculations under his breath; there were coupons, vouchers, of money invested, many things quite unintelligible to Helen. Sir John's fingers trembled with eagerness as he turned them over; there were various kinds of excitement and pleasure combined in his survey—pleasure in so much money recovered, for himself as well as his fellow-sufferers, fierce satisfaction in finding the culprit as bad as he hoped, the delight of being able to think and say "I told you so," all intensifying the pleasure of a new incident after long suspense. The two others looked on with very different feelings. Helen was not alive to the meaning of it all. She stood by even with a kind of consolation and gentle content in the thought that whatever wrong her father might have done would now be partially made up. She did not look at the face with which her lover regarded these discoveries, the disgust and pain and shame on his countenance conveyed no idea to her inexperience. She did not like Sir John, but she thought his exclamations, his looks of cruel elation, were only his disagreeable way of showing pleasure in the recovery of the money. She stood looking on for some time quite calmly. And then she said, "Will you divide it among the poorest people, please? He would have liked that best."

Sir John broke out with a fierce laugh. "No," he said rudely, "I cannot do sentimental injustice, Miss Helen. Your father had made a pretty provision for you, I must say; you ought to be obliged to his providence. But for this lucky chance, whoever suffered, he had very well feathered his nest."

"Harvey!" cried Ashton vehemently, "how can you speak before *her* of a lucky chance."

Sir John pushed back his chair farther from the table and looked at them. "I call it so," he said, "in every point of view. It is the best thing that could have happened for the man himself, and it is the highest luck for the children, and for you if you insist like a fool in connecting yourself with such a——"

"Silence!" thundered Charley making a step forward—"not another word!"

"I know nothing to prevent me saying as many words as I please," said Sir John, eyeing him with exasperating coolness.

Helen stood between the two excited men in the quiet of her innocence, not understanding for the first moment what their angry voices meant. Then her pale and almost passive face became transformed; slowly, gradually, the light rose in it, kindling her eyes, quickening the colour on her cheeks. She turned from one to the other, listening, entering into the meaning. At last she detached herself entirely from her lover, drawing her hand from his arm, and stood alone, with a kind of proud humility. She stopped till Sir John had made that last remark. His tone, the very sound of his voice filled her with wonder and dismay. She knew no reason for this hostility.

"My father is dead," she said with simple dignity; "if he has done wrong he is in God's hands; and we are two girls, fatherless and motherless. Is it with us you are angry, Sir John? It must be with me, for Janey is a child. What is it that I have done? If it is anything that I can put right, and you will tell me, I will do it. Why is it you look and speak to me so?"

Sir John was taken entirely aback. He looked at her and faltered. She put Charley away with her hand, with a smile and quivering lip. She would stand alone while he spoke to her.

"No," she said, "not you; do not come near me. Let him tell me what I have done wrong."

Sir John Harvey was a man of experience. He knew how to conduct himself in most emergencies. He was not apt to be put out. But when he found himself confronted by this young, solitary, friendless creature, who had but one person to stand by her in all the world, and he the one whom her powerful, prosperous enemy was endeavouring to detach from her, the courage and the strength was taken out of him. Sir John, so big and strong and well-to-do, faltered before the small, weak, desolate girl. He could not meet her eyes; his voice and his countenance failed him.

"I—I have nothing to say to you, Miss Goulburn," he said. "I did not approve of your father; he has made a great deal of mischief, and ruined many people; but he is dead, as you say. I don't pretend to judge you. The only thing is," he added, getting courage as he went on, "the only thing is—what you must see yourself—that a connection with you cannot do any man any good, that it must, in short, more or less, do harm. Your giving up this," he continued quickly, careless of Charley's loud interruption, "is very creditable to you. It will make everybody think better of you. Still, notwithstanding——"

"Helen, if you listen to that man, if you stand any longer and hear me insulted, I will think—I will believe you care for me no longer," Charley Ashton cried.

She looked from one to the other with tears in her eyes. "I have nobody in the world to tell me which is right," said Helen. She was far beyond shedding of tears, the moisture in her eyes was a powerful concentrated dew of suffering through which her troubled eyes looked out. At this moment there came another knock at the door, a quiet little knock low down, as of a creature of small stature, sounding against the lower panels; and then a small voice called from the same altitude, "Helen, Helen, open, Helen; I tan't open the door."

Sir John turned his face and his chair round towards the little voice, and sat there attentively expecting what was to come. Charley made one step to it and opened it, leaving the passage free. Janey appeared in the threshold in her black frock, her fair little face rising out of it like a flower, her little figure, so lightly poised, standing against the background of the panelled wall. She looked round upon them with the perfect calm of childhood. Then her eye was caught by the pocket-book on the table. Janey was not afraid of Sir John nor of any one in the wide world. She went up to the table and took the precious case into her little hands.

"This is Janey's fortune," she said, looking up with a smile into the face of the man beside her. "Are you doing to keep it safe for me?"

He sat and looked at her, helpless; he would have knocked down any man who had seized upon it—wrested it from the most powerful claimant; but before the little child he was helpless. He gazed at her blankly, stupidly, in the height of his dismay.

"I will not dive it to Sir John," said Janey, "because he does not look kind. He does not like Helen or me; he did not like papa; but I will dive it to Charley, for he is the one that is good. Catch, Charley!"

cried the little girl, throwing the precious case like a ball across the table. She clapped her hands when Ashton caught it with a laugh of childish pleasure. A ball or a fortune, what did it matter to Janey! "And look, Helen, who is coming!" the child said. "I was sent to tell you, but I forgot. Here she is coming! she is coming! and we are all doing home to our own house, and never to cry any more."

In another moment Helen's forlorn solitude, her helpless loneliness was over. She flew past Sir John, who rose stumbling to his feet, and Charley, who stood bewildered with Janey's fortune in his hand, and fell into the outstretched arms of a smiling and weeping woman who had come in after Janey, at the open door.

Doubt, and danger, and suspicion of herself and of everything around her, had been closing about Helen. She had looked round her vainly into the blackness and found no guidance, no one even to tell her what she ought to do. She had no mother, nor any friend that absolutely belonged to her; nevertheless, when she flew into Mrs. Ashton's arms, the world had settled down again out of those giddy whirlings and confused eccentricities. She did not know what she might be called upon to do or to give up; but life had taken its natural shape again

to the bewildered girl. She was not out of the labyrinth, but she had found the clue.

After the arrival of these strangers, Charley Ashton's father and step-mother, the village of Latour advanced daily in its knowledge of the ways of the English, a most curious and interesting study which gave great amusement to the cottagers. Mr. and Mrs. Ashton took the apartments in M. Goudron's house which had been so sadly vacated by l'Anglais, he who had escaped from all his pursuers by a night journey more sudden than any of his previous flights. The Latourois had been very sorry for the man who had died among them; but they were very glad, as was natural, to forget that tragical conclusion and to amuse themselves with all the difficulties about Monsieur's bath, and Madame's tea. The Curé looked with amused tolerance, yet contempt, at the costume of the clergyman, and at the droll pretences of that Protestant personage to be a priest like himself; and Madame Dupré, with an effort, for the sake of the benefactor who had liberated Baptiste, put up with the fastidiousness of the new visitors who turned up their noses at her *pot-au-feu*, and expected to find the refinements of the Trois Frères in the little *auberge*. "Talk of French cookery!" the new-comers cried; and they endeavoured to teach Margot how to "cook a joint" over her handful of charcoal, and to make English mustard out of the dark-complexioned powder which was all that was to be had in Latour. To see them walking about for ever, taking perpetual constitutionals, filled the villagers with wonder. But it would be impossible to describe the interest of Blanchette and Baptiste when there dawned upon them a pleasing certainty of the fate which was reserved for Mademoiselle. Little Blanchette was the one who had divined it from the first. The day M. Charles had come to the Château, that very day she had read it in his face. The loves of Cécile and Sir John afforded them no such sympathetic satisfaction. And, indeed, Sir John took his departure immediately, carrying with him the valuable case which held Janey's fortune. He washed his hands, he said, of the other matter. The Ashtons were on the spot to look after it for themselves, and if the father did not object to such a connection, of course it was no concern of his, who was merely a cousin. A cloud, a faint veil of separation, fell between Helen and the girls at the Château, in consequence of Sir John's opposition. Perhaps it gave Cécile her first experience of the difficulties that attend marriage with an Englishman. She did her best to be loyal both to her friend and her future husband, but the conflict was not without pain.

But what did any such paltry pain matter in the opening of the new day which came to Helen out of the clouds of the morning, sweet and dazzling in all the glories of life and spring? Her oldest friends put her hand into her lover's hand, and his father said the blessing over them. Let all the Sir Johns in the world object, what harm could it do?

They went to Paris and bought the bride her Indian outfit, she who had nothing. Helen's hundred a year had accumulated as her father had said. It came from her mother, and was honestly hers, and there was no reason why she should not use it. And it was at Paris that the young pair were married; and from thence that they set out to their distant home. But before they left Latour there was a pretty ceremony at which their presence was indispensable. Helen and little Janey put aside their black dresses and put on white ones to honour Blanchette's marriage. And when the religious ceremony took place, after the first day's performance at the Mairie, the bride herself, holding her husband by the hand, turned aside and led the way among all the iron crosses on the graves to the place where l'Anglais lay under a green mound, without any name. He had forfeited his name, his good fame, and honour. Nevertheless little Blanchette wept over the mound, and, kneeling down in her veil and myrtle crown, laid a white wreath upon the grass, and said a prayer for his soul. Did it do him any good in those dark countries whither the fugitive had taken flight "unhousel'd, disappointed, unanel'd?"

"Ma bonne, douce demoiselle," said Blanchette amid her tears, "how he was good to us, Monsieur votre père! Never shall a week pass when you are far, far away from Latour, but Baptiste and me, we will say a prayer for the repose of his soul."

The others said nothing, but stood silent about the nameless grave. What harm he had done, what suffering he had caused ! and yet he was but as other men, and gratitude gave him a prayer and a tear.